世图版对外汉语教材系列

中国百姓身边的故事

初中级汉语视听说教程（上）

Scenario Chinese

A Multi-skill Chinese Course
for Beginning
and Intermediate Students

（Ⅰ）

刘月华　　李金玉　　刘宪民　　葛良彦
Yuehua Liu　Jinyu Li　Xianmin Liu　Liangyan Ge　编著

世界图书出版公司

北京·广州·上海·西安

图书在版编目（CIP）数据

中国百姓身边的故事：初中级汉语视听说教程．上＝Scenario Chinese：A Multi-skill Chinese Course for Beginning and Intermediate Students．Ⅰ/刘月华等编著．—北京：世界图书出版公司北京公司，2008.3

ISBN 978-7-5062-8706-7

Ⅰ．中…　Ⅱ．刘…　Ⅲ．汉语-听说教学-对外汉语教学-教材　Ⅳ．H195.4

中国版本图书馆 CIP 数据核字（2007）第 170310 号

书　　名：	中国百姓身边的故事——初中级汉语视听说教程（上）	
编 著 者：	刘月华　李金玉　刘宪民　葛良彦	
责任编辑：	陈晓辉	
装帧设计：	盖雅设计	
图片提供：	田　琨	
出　　版：	世界图书出版公司北京公司	
发　　行：	世界图书出版公司北京公司	
	（北京朝内大街 137 号　邮编　100010　电话　64077922）	
销　　售：	各地新华书店和外文书店	
印　　刷：	北京高岭印刷有限公司	
开　　本：	787×1092 毫米　1/16　印张：13	
字　　数：	199 千字	
版　　次：	2008 年 3 月第 1 版　　2008 年 3 月第 1 次印刷	

ISBN 978-7-5062-8706-7/H・994　　　　　　　　定　价：40.00 元

前　言

　　我们在去年出版的《走进中国百姓生活——中高级汉语视听说教程》的前言中曾说："我们都是在美国多年从事中文教学的教师，深感目前能使学生通过真实鲜活的汉语了解中国现实社会的视听材料十分匮缺。为此我们编了这部教材。"《走进中国百姓生活》是中高级视听说教材，出于同样的目的，我们现在又编写了《中国百姓身边的故事》这套初中级视听说教材。我们一直在寻找篇幅短小、语言简易的现代中国电视剧，《咱老百姓》是先找到的，《身边的故事》是后找到的，所以根据这两个电视剧编写的教材《走进中国百姓生活》和《中国百姓身边的故事》也是程度高的先问世，程度低的后出版。这两套教材实际上是姊妹篇。据说中国一年在电视上播出上万集电视剧，但都是几十集乃至上百集的连续剧，电视短剧微乎其微。我们在《走进中国百姓生活》的前言中说："中国的电视剧很多，但是短剧可谓凤毛麟角。"到目前为止，我们只发现了《咱老百姓》和《身边的故事》两部短小的系列短剧。根据前者编写的《走进中国百姓生活》适合中文程度较高的学生，出版以来，受到广大师生的欢迎，而且已被韩国出版社引进。

　　《身边的故事》是北京电视台正在播放的电视短剧，每集5分钟，已播放了300多集。这部系列短剧把中国人身边正在发生的故事呈现在我们眼前。我们从中选了20个。这20个短剧反映了北京普通人生活的方方面面。剧中的人物有白领，有外地到北京的打工者，也有摊贩，还有外国旅游者；有老人，有孩子，还有盲人。剧中的人物多种多样，他们的生活色彩缤纷，他们的故事生动有趣。

　　《身边的故事》的语言也以日常口语为主，语言鲜活、生动。每集只有5分钟，无论作为辅助教材还是主教材，都会比较好用。

　　本教材每课包括课文、生词、练习几部分，练习突出了听说。

　　本教材的对象定位于中文程度为初级和中级的学习者。教师可以根据学生的程度和教学需要灵活安排进度。

　　美国戴维斯大学的储诚志教授用"中文助教"软件为我们挑选生词，使我们节省了很多时间。世界图书出版公司在本书出版过程中给与我们很多帮助，在此一并表示感谢。

刘月华　李金玉　刘宪民　葛良彦

PREFACE

In the preface to our *Reality Chinese : A Multi-skill Chinese Course for Intermediate and Advanced Students* published in 2006, we made this statement: "Having taught Chinese in the United States for many years, we were fully aware of the deficiency of the audio-video teaching materials that could help acquaint the students to the contemporary Chinese society through authentic and living language. Precisely because of that, we have compiled this textbook." Still for the same reason, we are now offering this volume of *Scenario Chinese : A Multi-skill Chinese Course for Beginning and Intermediate Students*. These two volumes form a series, even though we have not followed the usual order of publishing the lower-level textbook before the upper-level one.

Thousands of TV series are aired in China every year, but the vast majority of them are lengthy dramas with dozens of episodes. TV series of independent mini-plays are rare. So far we have only discovered two such series, *Folks Like You and Me* 咱老百姓 and *Stories Amid Ourselves* 身边的故事. The upper-level volume of our series consists of plays selected from *Folks Like You and Me*. Since its publication in 2006, it has been well received by teachers and students. Recently, it has been introduced into the Republic of Korea by a Korean press.

Stories Amid Ourselves is a series of mini-plays shown on Beijing Television. Over three hundred plays have been presented, from which we have selected twenty for this present volume. These twenty mini-plays, each lasting about five minutes duration, exhibit different scenarios in the metropolitan life in of Beijing. The characters include white-collar office workers, street peddlers, odd-jobbers from other parts of China, and tourists from foreign countries. Among them some are old and some are young, one is even blind. The plays feature a wide variety of characters whose lives are diverse and colorful and whose stories are vivacious and intriguing.

The plays collected here present vivid and up-to-date spoken Chinese. Since each mini-play conveniently functions as a unit, this volume can be used either as a principal or a supplementary textbook. Each unit includes the text, vocabulary, grammar notes, and exercises, which lay particular emphasis on listening and speaking. The book targets the beginning and intermediate students, and the instructors are encouraged to make adjustments of the pace according to the students' proficiency levels.

We are thankful to Professor Chu Chengzhi of University of California at Davis, who kindly helped us select vocabulary with his computer program "Chinese TA". Thanks are also due editors at the World Publishing Corporation (世界图书出版公司), whose assistance has been crucial in bringing this volume to print.

Liu Yuehua, Li Jinyu, Liu Xianmin, Ge Liangyan

《身边的故事》主题歌

The Theme Song of *Stories Amid Ourselves*

略　语　表

List of Abbreviations

adj.	Adjective	形容词
adv.	Adverb	副词
modal.	Modal verb	能愿动词
conj.	Conjunction	连词
interj.	Interjection	叹词
m.	Measure word	量词
n.	Noun	名词
N.	Proper Noun	专有名词
num.	Numerals	数词
ono.	Onomatopoeia	象声词
part.	Particle	助词
pron.	Pronoun	代词
prep.	Preposition	介词
t.	Time word	时间词
v.	Verb	动词
vc.	Verb plus complement	动补结构
vo.	Verb plus object	动宾结构

目 录

第一课 欢迎您再来

You Will Always Be Welcome Here

编剧：朱玉

人物（Characters）

赵大明（Zhào Dàmíng）——男，四十多岁，**出租车司机**。

玛　丽（Mǎlì）——女，三十多岁，美国**游客**。

课　文　Text

玛　丽：No，No。

赵大明：**哟**，您不是要吃饭吗？这就是外国朋友们**经常**吃饭的**地**儿？

玛　丽：我来中国是**旅游**，我不要吃西餐，我要吃中国最好吃的**食品**。

1. 出租车	chūzūchē	n.	taxi
2. 司机	sījī	n.	driver; chauffeur
3. 游客	yóukè	n.	traveller; tourist; sightseer
4. 哟	yō	interj.	(expressing slight surprise)
5. 经常	jīngcháng	adv.	often; regularly
6. 地儿	dìr	n.	place (colloq.)
7. 旅游	lǚyóu	v.	travel; tour
8. 食品	shípǐn	n.	food

赵大明：您这**汉语**说得**倍儿棒**[N1]啊！

玛　丽：我是个**教师**，我在美国教汉语。

赵大明：这么说您是一个**中国通**啊，行，您想吃什么，告诉我，我给您送过去。

玛　丽：不知道。

赵大明：太**逗**了，您自己想吃什么您都不知道啊。

玛　丽：是的，因为北京好吃的东西太多了，我想不好[N2]。

赵大明：小姐，您是教汉语的，没来过中国啊？

玛　丽：我来过中国，可是，我没有来过北京。

赵大明：**噢，这么着**[N3]，让我给您介绍一下，外国朋友到北京有"三必须"。

玛　丽："三必须"？哪三个必须啊？

赵大明：必须到**长城**，必须**游故宫**，必须得吃**烤鸭**！

玛　丽：烤鸭！我就吃烤鸭！It's a good idea！（好主意！）

玛　丽：你看，烤——鸭——店！

---

9. 汉语	Hànyǔ	N.	Chinese language
10. 倍儿	bèir	adv.	extremely; exceptionally (colloq.)
11. 教师	jiàoshī	n.	teacher
12. 中国通	Zhōngguó tōng	n.	old China hand
13. 逗	dòu	adj./v.	amusing, funny; amuse
14. 噢	ō	interj.	(suggesting surprised understanding)
15. 这么着	zhèmezhe	pron.	in that case
16. 长城	Chángchéng	N.	Great Wall
17. 游	yóu	v.	tour; sightsee
18. 故宫	Gùgōng	N.	Imperial Palace
19. 烤鸭	kǎoyā	n.	roast duck
20. 烤鸭店	kǎoyā diàn	n.	roast duck restaurant

赵大明：这个呀，是**便宜坊**烤鸭店，我**今**儿带您去的是**全聚德**烤
　　　　鸭店。

玛　丽：这**两家**的**鸭子**有什么不一样吗？

赵大明：他们两家的鸭子是一样的，就是**做法**不一样。全聚德做的
　　　　是**挂炉烤鸭**······

玛　丽：什么叫挂炉？

赵大明：这挂炉烤鸭呀，就是把鸭子放在**炉火上烤**，烤出来的鸭子
　　　　清香油亮，**外焦里嫩**，便宜坊的是闷炉烤，烤出来的口味，
　　　　还^{N4}真跟全聚德的不一样！

21.	便宜坊	Biànyífāng	N.	(name of a restaurant)
22.	今儿	jīnr	t.	today (colloq.)
23.	全聚德	Quánjùdé	N.	(name of a restaurant)
24.	家	jiā	m.	(measure word for business establishments)
25.	鸭子	yāzi	n.	duck; duckling
26.	做法	zuò·fǎ①	n.	way of doing or making something
27.	挂炉	guàlú	n.	(a kind of stove for roasting duck)
28.	炉火	lúhuǒ	n.	stove fire
29.	烤	kǎo	v.	bake; roast; toast; broil
30.	清香	qīngxiāng	adj.	delicately fragrant
31.	油亮	yóuliàng	adj.	shiny; glossy
32.	外焦里嫩	wài jiāo lǐ nèn		burnt outside but tender inside
33.	闷炉	mènlú	n.	(a kind of stove for roasting duck)
34.	口味	kǒuwèi	n.	(of food) taste; flavor

---

① 既可读轻声，也可读原调的字，注音时上标调号，注音前加圆点，后同。

玛　丽：哦，这就是全聚德吗？

赵大明：对呀。

玛　丽：太漂亮了！太漂亮了！像宫殿一样的，我太高兴了，谢谢您，赵先生！

赵大明：**不客气**，我祝[N5]您**胃口**好，明儿呀，我再**拉**您到便宜坊，**尝**尝他们的闷炉烤鸭。

玛　丽：**唉**，谢谢！谢谢！

赵大明：好，**慢用**[N6]。

玛　丽：再见。

玛　丽：赵先生，你好快呀！谢谢你。

35.	宫殿	gōngdiàn	n.	palace
36.	不客气	bú kèqì		you are welcome
37.	胃口	wèikǒu	n.	appetite
38.	拉	lā	v.	(of a driver) drive (somebody)
39.	尝	cháng	v.	taste; try the flavor of
40.	唉	ài	interj.	(model particle indicating a response)
41.	慢用	màn yòng		eat casually; take your time

赵大明：别客气了，**咱们**算^{N7}**老朋友**啦，快**上车**吧！**坐好**啊！

赵大明：玛丽小姐，这几天在北京玩儿得怎么样？

玛　丽：太棒了，长城、故宫都去了，啊，对了，烤鸭也吃了，你说的"三必须"，我都"必须"了。

赵大明：北京这么多好吃的，都吃什么了？

玛　丽：有烤鸭、**涮羊肉**、饺子……还有……**圆**圆的……**月亮**！

赵大明：月亮？……哦，是**月饼**吧？

玛　丽：对，月饼。

赵大明：中国的**美食**多，**故事**也多，你就拿最简单的吃**面条儿**来说^{N8}吧，这就有**讲究**^{N9}。

玛　丽：什么讲究？

赵大明：过去的老北京，过生日的时候不**兴**^{N10}吃**蛋糕**，**寿星老儿**得吃面条儿。

42.	咱们	zánmen	pron.	we; us (including the listener)
43.	老朋友	lǎo péngyou		old friend
44.	上车	shàng chē	vo.	get in the car (or on the bus or train)
45.	坐好	zuò hǎo	vc.	get seated properly
46.	涮羊肉	shuàn yángròu		instant-boiled mutton
47.	圆	yuán	adj.	round
48.	月亮	yuèliang	n.	the moon
49.	月饼	yuèbing	n.	moon cake
50.	美食	měishí	n.	delicious food; delicacies
51.	故事	gùshi	n.	story
52.	面条儿	miàntiáor	n.	noodles
53.	讲究	jiǎngjiu	v./n.	pay attention to; be particular about; be fussy about
54.	兴	xīng	v.	have (something)in vogue
55.	蛋糕	dàngāo	n.	cake
56.	寿星老儿	shòuxīnglǎor	n.	person whose birthday is being celebrated

玛　丽：为什么？

赵大明：面条儿不是**细长**吗，它就**象征**着**长寿**，吃了这面以后就能**长命百岁**。

玛　丽：你说面条儿我还真的**有点儿**饿，我现在想吃北京的**炸酱面**。

赵大明：不就是想吃炸酱面吗？[N11]这事简单……

赵大明：请吧。

玛　丽：哎，这是什么饭店？

赵大明：这不是什么[N12]饭店，这是我们家。我今儿呀**替**您**做回主**，我请您尝尝**咱**北京**老百姓**的第一**名吃**——炸酱面。我妈是个**老北京**，她做的那炸酱面比饭馆儿还**地道**，希望您喜欢，您别客气，今儿我请您！

玛　丽：好。

赵大明：请。

57.	细	xì	adj.	fine; thin
58.	象征	xiàngzhēng	v.	symbolize; signify
59.	长寿	chángshòu	adj.	long life; longevity
60.	长命百岁	cháng mìng bǎi suì		live to be hundred years old
61.	有点儿	yǒudiǎnr	adv.	a little bit; somewhat
62.	炸酱面	zhájiàngmiàn	n.	noodles in fried bean sauce
63.	替	tì	prep.	take the place of; substitue for
64.	做回主	zuò huí zhǔ	vo.	make the decision for（somebody）
65.	咱	zán	pron.	we, us; I, me
66.	百姓	bǎixìng	n.	common people
67.	名吃	míngchī	n.	famous food
68.	老北京	lǎo běijīng		person who has lived in Beijing for a long time and knows the city thoroughly
69.	地道	dìdao	adj.	genuine; authentic

赵大明：来来来。

玛　丽：北京好，北京的出租车司机也好，你，哦，不不不，您，
　　　　非常**热情**，还有学问……

赵大明：**您太客气了！实话跟您说**[N13]，像我这样的出租司机，北京
　　　　多着呢[N14]！

玛　丽：以后我还要来北京。

赵大明：好啊，欢迎您再来！

玛　丽：一定，一定再来。

赵大明：来来。

70. 热情	rèqíng	adj.	passionate; warm-hearted
71. 有学问	yǒu xuéwen		knowledgeable
72. 实话跟您说	shíhuà gēn nín shuō		tell you the truth
73. 着呢	zhene	part.	(following an adjective to indicate degree) very; quite; greatly

注释　Notes

1. **"倍儿（棒）"：**

   "倍儿"有加倍的意思，表示极高的程度，有"非常、极其"的意思。北京口语。"倍儿棒"就是"非常好"的意思。"棒"是北方口语。

   "倍儿" literally means "doubly" of "several times". It often carries the meaning of "extremely" or "exceptionally". As a Beijing slang，"倍儿棒" simply means "exceptionally good". Other examples of the use of "倍儿" include：

   (1) 您这汉语说得倍儿棒啊！

   Your Chinese is exceptionally good!

   (2) 今天的电影倍儿好看，你没看太可惜了。

   Today's movie was extremely good. It was a shame you didn't watch it.

   (3) 那个地方夏天倍儿热。

   Summer is extremely hot in that place.

   再如：Other examples：

   倍儿快（extremely fast）　　　倍儿多（an enormous number of）

   倍儿有意思（extremely interesting）　倍儿贵（extremely expensive）

   倍儿乱（extremely chaotic）

2. **结果补语"好"：**

   补语"好"表示某一个动作的完成，即为下一步动作做了准备，有可以开始下一个动作的意思。

   The resultative complement "好"：As a complement，"好" indicates the completion of an action，which is often a prerequisite for another action to take place.

   (1) 玛丽：因为北京好吃的东西太多了，我想不好。

   　　 Mary：There are too many delicacies in Beijing. I don't know what to choose.

   　　 这个句子表示玛丽想了要吃什么，但是还没有做出决定（这里"想不好"，应该是"没想好"）。如果她想清楚了，就是"想好"了，她就可以去吃了。

The sentence suggests that Mary has not reached a decision after thinking about her choice. Once she does（"想好"）, it will be time for her to eat.

（2）快上车吧！坐好啊！（坐好了就可以开车了）

Get on the bus quickly and be seated.（Once you are seated the bus will leave）

（3）老师：现在我们听写，笔和纸准备好了吗？

Teacher：Now we will have a dictation. Are you ready with your pens and paper?

（4）饭做好了，快来吃吧。

Dinner is ready. Come quickly and eat.

3. **"这么着"：**

意思是"这样"，在这里起连接句子的作用。口语。

As a colloquial expression，"这么着" like "这样"（so，in that case），serves here as a link for two adjacent sentences.

（1）玛丽：我来过中国，可是，我没有来过北京。

Mary：I was in China before, but this is my first time to be in Beijing.

赵大明：噢，这么着，让我给您介绍一下，外国朋友到北京有"三必须"。

Zhao Daming：Oh，in that case，let me give you some kind of an orientation. Friends from other countries have three "must do's" in Beijing.

在这个句子里，赵大明说"这么着"，意思是"既然你没有来过北京，这样吧，我给你介绍一下……"。在这里，"这么着"就把后边的句子和前边的句子连接起来了。

When Zhao Daming says "这么着"，what he suggests is："Since this is your first visit to Beijing，I will give you some kind of an orientation. . . ". "这么着" thus links up what Mary has said and what he is going to say.

4. **"还"（一）：**

表示出乎意料的语气，有时有赞美的意思。在"便宜坊的是闷炉烤，烤出来的口味，还真跟全聚德的不一样"这个句子里，说话人用"还"表示正在说的事情会使听话人玛丽出乎意料。再如：

"还" denotes a tone of surprise，and it sometimes suggests an approving attitude. In the sentence——"便宜坊的是闷炉烤，烤出来的口味，还真跟

全聚德的不一样", "还" suggests that what is being said could sound surprising to the listener, Mary. Other examples include:

(1) 外边下着大雨，我以为你不回来了，没想到你还真的来了。

It was raining heavily and I thought you wouldn't be back. Who would have expected you to be here!

(2) 这么难的问题你还回答得很好，真不错。

It was such a difficult question and you answered really well. Simply remarkable!

5. "祝":

口头或书面表示祝愿时可以说。

"祝" appears in different salutations and congratulatory formulas, oral or written.

(1) 祝您胃口好！（吃饭前）　　　　Have a good appetite! (Before a meal)

(2) 祝旅途愉快！（旅行送别）　　　　Bon voyage! (Sending some off)

(3) 祝一路平安！　　　　Have a safe journey!

(4) 祝身体健康！　　　　I wish you good health!

(5) 祝生日快乐！　　　　Happy birthday!

(6) 祝圣诞快乐！　　　　Merry Christmas!

(7) 祝新年快乐！　　　　Happy New Year!

6. "慢用":

服务人员在客人开始吃饭前，为了表示客气、礼貌，可以说："请慢用！"

Before the customers start to eat, the waiter or waitress may say "请慢用" (literally, "Please take your time to eat") to show his or her politeness.

和别人一起吃饭时，如果你先吃完了，也可以对还没有吃完的人说："请慢用"或者"慢慢吃"。

If you finished your meal before your fellow diners, you can also say to them: "请慢用" or "慢慢吃".

送别客人时，可以说："慢走！"

When seeing a visitor off, it is customary to say: "慢走" (literally, "Walk at a casual pace").

7. "算":

意思是：说话人认为可以说"是"或者"当做"。

"算" means, from the speaker's perspective, "being equivalent to" or "being able to be considered as". Examples：

(1) 咱们算老朋友啦。

We consider each other an old friend.

(2) 他算是我的学生吧，常来问我数学问题。

I count him as a student，as he often comes to ask me math questions.

(3) 这个相机是我太太的，送给你，算是我给你的礼物吧。

This camera is my wife's. You can consider it as my present to you.

8. "拿……来说"：

"拿"有"用"的意思，"拿……来说"用丁举例说明。

In the structure "拿……来说"，"拿" carries a meaning similar to "use". The structure is often used when citing examples，e. g.：

(1) 中国的美食多，故事也多，你就拿最简单的吃面条儿来说吧，这就有讲究。

There are many varieties of Chinese cuisine，and many stories as well. Take the simplest food，noodles. There are details here that call for special attention.

(2) 我们班的同学兴趣都不太一样，拿我的好朋友大伟来说，他喜欢听音乐，可是我不喜欢听音乐，我喜欢打球。

Students in our class have different interests. For example，my good friend Dawei likes music，but I don't. I like to play ball instead.

9. "(有) 讲究"：

"讲究"有重视的意思。口语。

"讲究" is a colloquialism that means "to pay particular attention to" or "to attach importance to".

(1) 应该教育小学生讲究文明礼貌。

Elementary school students should be taught to be civil and polite.

(2) 他很讲究吃。

He is particular about eating.

如果说某人"讲究吃"，意思是他重视与"吃"有关的一些方面，比如质量、营养或者餐具等等。如果说某人"讲究穿"，意思是他重视与"穿"有关的一些方面，比如服饰的质量、样式等等。

The expression "讲究吃" suggests paying much attention to different aspects of eating，such as the quality and nutrition of the food，the types of the tableware，etc. Similarly，the expression "讲究穿" denotes a strong interest in various aspects of clothing such as its quality and fashions.

"讲究"也是名词，意思是值得重视、注意的地方。如：

"讲究" can also be used as a noun，which means things that one should attach importance or pay particular attention to：

（3）中国人送礼有很多讲究。

The Chinese pay a lot of attention to the details of presenting gifts.

本课的"有讲究"中的"讲究"是名词。

In the current lesson，"讲究" appears as a noun.

10. **"兴"：**

"流行"的意思，多用于穿着打扮，也可以用于某种风俗习惯。口语。

"兴" as a colloquialism，means "to have（something）in the vogue". It is often used in reference to fashions，but can also refer to social customs and folkways.

（1）今年兴短裙。

Short skirts are the vogue this year.

（2）现在又开始兴披肩了。

The cape is fashionable again nowadays.

（3）过生日的时候不兴吃疙瘩汤。

One is not supposed to have noodle-lump soup for his birthday.

11. **反问句（一）：**

有些句子形式上是疑问句，但是不要求听话人回答，而是表示说话人的一种看法。反问句比同样意思的陈述句更具有表现力，语气更强。一般来说，肯定形式的反问句表示否定的意思，否定形式的反问句表示肯定的意思。更为复杂的反问句，我们这里就不涉及了。

Rhetorical questions（I）：A rhetorical question is one that does not require an answer from the listener but only suggests the opinion of the speaker. Often it is more expressive and carries a stronger tone than a statement. A formally positive rhetorical question is actually negative in meaning，and a formally negative one is positive in meaning. There are，however，more complicated rhetorical questions，which are beyond our scope here.

（1）不就是想吃炸酱面吗？（意思：你就想吃炸酱面，对吗？）

Isn't that you just want to eat noodles in fried bean sauce?（I know you want noodles in fried bean sauce.）

（2）我说的难道不对吗？（意思：我说得很对。）

Am I not telling the truth? (I am telling the truth!)

（3）我这样说，错了吗？（意思：我这样说没错。）

Did I say anything wrong? (I didn't say anything wrong.)

12. **"什么"**：

用在引述别人的话前，表示不同意那种说法。

"什么" can be used before a word or phrase cited from someone else, and indicate a rebuttal.

（1）这不是什么饭店，这是我们家。

This is not some kind of hotel—it's our home!

（2）A：听说他人很好。

I heard he is a good guy.

B：他不是什么好人，不要跟他交朋友。

He is not a good guy at all! Don't make friends with him.

（3）A：他最近赚了很多钱，真棒！

He has made a lot of money recently. It's indeed wonderful!

B：钱太多了，我看不是什么好事。

In my opinion, having too much money is not a good thing at all.

13. **"实话跟您说"**：

为了让对方相信自己说的，可以说"实话跟你说，……"，也可以说"实话告诉你……"。

The structure "实话跟你（您）说" or "实话告诉你" literally means "to tell you the truth". It is often used to make one's words sound more convincing to the listener.

（1）实话跟您说，像我这样的出租司机，北京多着呢！

To be honest with you, there are countless cab drivers like me in Beijing!

（2）实话告诉你，我从来不喜欢这个人。

To tell you the truth, I've never liked that person.

（3）实话跟您说，我今天还没吃饭呢，过一会儿再帮您修理电脑吧。

To be honest with you, I haven't eaten anything yet today. Give me a moment，and then I will fix the computer for you.

14. **"着呢"**：

表示较高的程度，有"非常"的意思。用在形容词或表示心理活动的

动词后，北方口语。

　　As a northern colloquialism，"着呢" follows an adjective or a verb that indicates a mental activity. It suggests a relatively high degree, and therefore has a meaning similar to the adverb "非常"，which，however，precedes the adjective or verb instead.

（1）像我这样的出租司机，北京多着呢！

　　Cab drivers like me—there are too many in Beijing！

（2）我今天累着呢。

　　I'm really tired today.

（3）很久没回家了，我想家着呢。

　　I haven't been home for a long time and I am quite homesick now.

听说练习　Listening & Speaking Exercises

■ **一、课文理解 Text Comprehension**

（一）根据故事情节选择适当的答案

Please choose the most appropriate answer based on the story

1. 玛丽来中国是为了（　　　）

    A. 吃最好吃的食品　　　B. 旅游　　　　　　C. 教汉语

2. 玛丽以前来过（　　　）

    A. 中国　　　　　　　　B. 北京　　　　　　C. 全聚德烤鸭店

3. 赵大明说外国朋友到北京有"三必须"，请从下面选出三个"必须"
（　　　）

    A. 坐出租、去长城、吃饺子

    B. 吃烤鸭、游故宫、去长城

    C. 吃月饼、游长城、吃烤鸭

4. 赵大明把玛丽送到全聚德，玛丽很高兴，因为（　　　）

    A. 饭店很漂亮　　　　B. 饭店是宫殿　　　　C. 饭店很便宜

5. 便宜坊烤鸭店和全聚德烤鸭店做的烤鸭（　　　）

    A. 不一样　　　　　　B. 一样　　　　　　　C. 差不多

6. 玛丽认为北京的出租车司机（　　　）

    A. 热情但没有学问

    B. 有学问但不够热情

    C. 又热情又有学问

（二）根据课文判断下面句子意思的正误

State whether the following statements are true or false based on the story

1.（　　　）玛丽在中国教过汉语。

2.（　　　）全聚德烤鸭店大得像宫殿一样。

3.（　　　）赵大明做的炸酱面比饭馆儿还地道。

4.（　　）玛丽不知道北京有哪些好吃的东西。

5.（　　）全聚德做的是挂炉烤鸭，清香油亮、外焦里嫩。

6.（　　）赵大明是一位又热情又有学问的出租车司机。

7.（　　）玛丽和赵大明是老朋友，他们认识很长时间了。

8.（　　）赵大明家开饭店。

（三）先听故事叙述，然后复述故事

Listen to the narrative first and then retell the story

　　玛丽是一位美国汉语教师。他虽然来过中国，但是到北京来还是第一次。出租车司机赵大明对她很热情，告诉她外国朋友到北京都要有"三必须"，就是必须到长城、必须游故宫、必须吃烤鸭。

　　赵大明给她介绍了北京有名的两家烤鸭店，一家叫全聚德，一家叫便宜坊，并且告诉她全聚德的烤鸭和便宜坊的口味不一样。

　　在赵大明的帮助下，玛丽不但去了长城和故宫，还吃了中国最好吃的食品：北京烤鸭、涮羊肉、饺子、月饼和赵大明妈妈做的地道的北京炸酱面。

　　玛丽喜欢北京，更喜欢像赵大明那样又热情又有学问的出租车司机。

（四）回答问题

Answer the following questions

1. 赵大明和玛丽是哪国人？他们在什么地方？他们是做什么的？

2. 玛丽为什么不知道自己想吃什么？

3. 玛丽以前到过中国吗？来过北京吗？

4. 赵大明说外国人到北京必须做哪三件事？

5. 赵大明说了北京几个烤鸭店的名字？你能记住这些烤鸭店的名字吗？说说看。

6. 赵大明说，全聚德烤鸭店和便宜坊烤鸭店烤出来的鸭子都有什么特色？

8. 玛丽在北京都吃了哪些东西？这些东西你吃过吗？

9. 赵大明说中国人过生日讲究吃什么？为什么？

10. 赵大明在哪儿请玛丽吃的炸酱面？为什么？

二、词语使用 Application of Vocabulary and Grammar

（一）选择题

Choose the item that is grammatically correct

1. 别客气了，咱们＿＿＿＿＿老朋友啦，快上车吧！坐好啊！

　　A. 真　　　　　　　B. 就　　　　　　　C. 算

2. 北京这么多好吃的，_____吃什么了？

    A. 都   B. 就   C. 想

3. 便宜坊的是闷炉烤，烤_____的口味，还真跟全聚德的不一样！

    A. 上来   B. 出来   C. 起来

4. 过去的老北京，过生日的时候不_____吃蛋糕，寿星老儿得吃面条儿。

    A. 用   B. 兴   C. 都

5. 这不是什么饭店，这是我们家。我今儿呀_____您做回主，我请您尝尝咱北京老百姓的第一名吃——炸酱面。

    A. 替   B. 请   C. 把

6. 您太客气了！实话跟您说，像我这样的出租司机，北京多_____呢！

    A. 极   B. 着   C. 很

（二）选择题

Circle the answer that best reflects the meaning of the underlined portion of the sentence

1. 赵大明说玛丽是一个<u>中国通</u>。（　　）

    A. 玛丽常来中国

    B. 玛丽对中国很了解

    C. 玛丽中文说得很流利

2. 赵大明说玛丽汉语说得<u>倍儿棒</u>。（　　）

    A. 比他快

    B. 非常好

    C. 太多

3. <u>太逗了</u>，您自己想吃什么您都不知道。（　　）

    A. 很不聪明

    B. 你太爱开玩笑了

    C. 真有意思

4. 赵大明对玛丽说："行，您想吃什么，告诉我，<u>我给您送过去</u>。"（　　）

    A. 我买了送给你吃

    B. 我开车送你去饭馆儿

C. 我让太太做了送给你吃

5. 听了赵大明说外国朋友到北京必须得吃烤鸭，玛丽说："烤鸭！我就吃烤鸭！"（　　）

    A. 我决定吃烤鸭了

    B. 你吃烤鸭我就吃

    C. 好吧，我就去吃烤鸭

（三）读例句，按照例句用提供的词语造句

Read the model sentence and make sentences with the provided topics or words

1. 您这汉语说得倍儿棒啊！学了多少年了？

    （1）她中国饭做得_____

    （2）今天的电影_____

    （3）那个地方夏天_____

    （4）他哥那人_____

    （5）那个店的东西_____

    （6）你英语说得_____

2. 在下面的情境中你应该说什么？

    What would you say in the following situations?（Using either 祝……or 慢＋Verb）

    （1）吃饭前说：_____

    （2）在机场送朋友说：_____

    （3）向别人敬酒时说：_____

    （4）参加朋友生日晚会说：_____

    （5）过中国新年时说：_____

    （6）先吃完饭，对同桌一起吃饭的人说：_____

    （7）送客人走时说：_____

3. 中国的美食多，故事也多，你就拿最简单的吃面条来说吧，这就有讲究。

    （1）北京的司机真好，_____

    （2）中国有意思的地方不少，_____

    （3）美国人汉语说得很好的人不少，_____

    （4）中国人过新年跟西方人过的圣诞节差不多，_____

4. 玛丽：你说面条儿我还真的有点儿饿，我现在想吃北京的炸酱面。

    （1）累……走不动了，……

（2）酒……有两瓶，……

  （3）帮你找女朋友……认识两位小姐，……

  （4）要借床……有一张，……

  （5）吃烤鸭……有兴趣，……

5. 你不就是想吃炸酱面吗？这事简单……

  （1）想去长城，＿＿＿＿＿＿＿＿＿＿＿＿＿

  （2）想吃烤鸭，＿＿＿＿＿＿＿＿＿＿＿＿＿

  （3）想吃中国饭，＿＿＿＿＿＿＿＿＿＿＿＿

  （4）想交中国朋友，＿＿＿＿＿＿＿＿＿＿＿

  （5）想吃蛋糕，＿＿＿＿＿＿＿＿＿＿＿＿＿

6. 地道

  （1）这家饭馆儿的厨师都是从中国请来的，＿＿＿＿＿＿＿

  （2）他是上海人，但是普通话＿＿＿＿＿＿＿＿＿＿＿

  （3）我是南京人，北京菜＿＿＿＿＿＿＿＿＿＿＿＿

  （4）赵大明的母亲是老北京，＿＿＿＿＿＿＿＿＿＿＿

7. ～ 着呢

  （1）像赵大明那样的出租车司机，＿＿＿＿＿＿＿＿＿

  （2）帮朋友搬了一天家，现在我＿＿＿＿＿＿＿＿＿＿

  （3）现在别问我问题，我＿＿＿＿＿＿＿＿＿＿＿＿

  （4）他嘴上说不着急找女朋友，其实他＿＿＿＿＿＿＿＿

（四）用"兴" or "不兴" 改说下列句子

Paraphrase the following sentences with "兴" or "不兴"

1. 过去的老北京，过生日的时候没有吃蛋糕的，一般都吃面条儿，象征着长命百岁。

2. 中国人结婚时新娘要穿红的，而西方人要穿白的。

3. 20 世纪 80 年代很多男人都留长发，现在很多男青年都剃光头了。

4. 现在中国人也买鲜花送人了。

（五）用"实话跟您说" 开头回答下列问题

Provide your replay starting with "实话跟您说"

1. 你对旅行没兴趣，是不是？

2. 你这次考试怎么考得这么糟？

3. 你不爱他吗？

4. 玛丽的汉语真是说得那么好吗？

5. 你真的很喜欢开出租车这种工作吗？

6. 你男朋友的妈妈真的那么好吗？

（六）角色扮演 Role play

Make a dialogue with a classmate. One party plays the tourist，and the other plays the cab driver. Your dialogue should incorporate the provided items.

旅客	出租车司机
You've been to China，but this is the first time you are visiting Beijing. You tell the cab driver what you wish to do while in Beijing. At the end of your trip，you want to express to the cab driver that you are much impressed by his knowledge of Beijing and very appreciative of his hospitality.	You are impressed by the tourist's proficiency in Chinese. You give her advice on visiting Beijing. Hearing the tourist's compliment，you tell her that you are just an ordinary cab driver in Beijing.
1. 教师　　2. 汉语　　3. 旅游 4. 我不要……，要…… 5. 想不好　6. 有什么不一样 7. 热情　　8. 学问	1. V 得倍儿棒　　2. 中国通 3. 太逗了　　　　4. 介绍 5. "三必须"　　　6. 实话跟您说 7. 像……　　　　8. 多着呢

■ 三、课堂讨论 Discussion

1. 你遇见过像赵大明这样的出租车司机吗？玛丽对北京和北京的出租车司机印象怎么样？

2. 你去过中国吗？如果去过，坐过出租车吗？你对中国的出租车司机的印象怎样？

3. 在你看来，赵大明很热爱他的职业吗？做出租车司机这种工作有什么好处和坏处？

4. 谈谈你接触过的最好的和最坏的出租车司机。

四、Challenge yourself to learn more about China

利用互联网对下列问题做一些社会调查，把你调查到的情况在班上向同学们作一个汇报。

1. 北京普通蓝领工人月工资是多少？白领工作人员呢？

2. 在北京，一位出租车司机一个月一般可以挣多少钱？他们的收入算很低吗？

3. 在你们国家，什么样的人做出租车司机这样的工作？人们对这种职业有什么看法？

第二课 十元钱

Ten Yuan

 编剧：尤欣

人物（Characters）

王大爷（Wáng dàye）

王大爷的老伴儿（Wáng dàye de lǎobànr）

小伙子（xiǎohuǒzi）

课 文 Text

路　人：王大爷，您早！

王大爷：回来啦。

小伙子：大爷，早。

王大爷：怎么了，修车啊？

---

1. 钱	qián	n.	money
2. 大爷	dàye	n.	uncle (a respectful form of address for an elderly man); father's elder brother
3. 老伴儿	lǎobànr	n.	husband or wife (of an old married couple)
4. 小伙子	xiǎohuǒzi	n.	lad; young fellow
5. 怎么了	zěnme le		What happened? What's the matter?
6. 修车	xiū chē	vo.	repair bike; fix bike

小伙子：不是，我啊，跟您**商量**个事儿，我**早晨着急**，我把**钱包、钥匙**都**锁**家里了，我这**兜**里一分钱都没带[N1]，我着急去**采访**去，您能借我十块钱吗？

王大爷：什么？**管**我借十块钱？

小伙子：您不认识我啊？我这车都在您这儿修的，我就住**后面**那个3号楼。

王大爷：就那黄楼？

小伙子：对，对，我就借十块钱，下了班我就给您还回来，行吗？大爷。

王大爷：十块钱够吗？

小伙子：够了，够了！我**下班**就给您还回来。谢谢大爷啊。

王大爷：这小伙子！

老　伴：回来了？**赶紧**吃饭吧。今天啊我做了你最**爱**吃的**红烧排骨**。

7. 商量	shāngliang	v.	discuss; talk over with sb.
8. 早晨	zǎochén	t.	morning
9. 着急	zháojí	adj.	worried; anxious
10. 钱包	qiánbāo	n.	purse; wallet
11. 钥匙	yàoshi	n.	key
12. 锁	suǒ	v./n.	lock
13. 兜	dōu	n.	pocket
14. 采访	cǎifǎng	v.	interview
15. 管	guǎn	prep.	from (sb.)
16. 后面	hòumian	n.	at the back; behind
17. 下班	xià bān	vo.	get off work
18. 赶紧	gǎnjǐn	adv.	hurry up
19. 爱	ài	v.	like; be fond of
20. 红烧	hóngshāo	v.	braise (meat)
21. 排骨	páigǔ	n.	spareribs

王大爷：哟，今天是什么日子这是？^{N2}

老 伴：什么日子也不是，我看你一天在**外面**修车**挺**累的，给你**解
解馋，补补**^{N3}。

王大爷：还是^{N4}我老伴儿知道**心疼**我呀。

老 伴：哎，那你今天**挣**了几**壶**酒钱？

王大爷：你一^{N5}**提**这钱，我**想起来**了，今天早上有个小伙子，管我
借了十块钱。

老 伴：**咳**，我说你又**冒傻气**^{N6}，都不认识人家就^{N7}把钱借出去？

王大爷：我看那小伙今天早晨挺着急的，他不像是个**骗子**啊。

老 伴：**哼**，你等着**瞧吧，肯定没下文**^{N8}了。

22. 日子	rìzi	n.	day; days
23. 外面	wài·miàn	n.	outside
24. 挺	tǐng	adv.	very; rather
25. 解馋	jiě chán	vo.	(see note 3)
26. 补	bǔ	v.	nourish body; make up for
27. 心疼	xīnténg	v.	love dearly; feel sorry
28. 挣	zhèng	v.	earn
29. 壶	hú	n.	kettle; pot
30. 提	tí	v.	mention about
31. 想起来	xiǎng qilai	vc.	recall; remember
32. 咳	hāi	interj.	(an exclamation)
33. 冒傻气	mào shǎqì	vo.	(see note 6)
34. 人家	rénjia	pron.	sb. else; other people
35. 骗子	piànzi	n.	swindler; cheater
36. 哼	hēng	interj.	hmph
37. 瞧	qiáo	v.	look
38. 肯定	kěndìng	adv.	certainly; definitely
39. 下文	xiàwén	n.	(see note 8)

老　伴：哎，我说你也别**瞎琢磨**了，不就十块钱吗？**只当**它**打水漂**[N9]了。

王大爷：你说得**倒轻巧**，挣十块钱那么容易吗？

老　伴：那你还为这十块钱琢磨出点儿病来**不成**？你呀，以后长点儿**心眼**儿[N10]就**结了**[N11]。喝着，我给你**盛**饭去。

小伙子：大爷，借**扳子使**一下儿，啊。

王大爷：用吧。是你呀小伙子，你忘了你管我借十块钱？

小伙子：大爷，**不好意思**[N12]，我……我忘了我[N13]，大爷，您拿着。

王大爷：是二十的呀，我刚出**摊**儿，没钱找你。

小伙子：还找什么呀大爷，您拿着吧，是我忘了，不好意思啊。

王大爷：**哎呀**，我**差点**儿**冤枉**了这个小伙子。

40.	瞎	xiā	adv.	groundlessly; foolishly
41.	琢磨	zuómo	v.	ponder; think over
42.	（只）当	(zhǐ) dàng	v.	take (sth. as...)
43.	打水漂	dǎ shuǐpiāo	vo.	(see note 9)
44.	倒	dào	adv.	(indicating that sth. is not what one thinks)
45.	轻巧	qīng·qiǎo	adj.	simple; easy
46.	不成	bùchéng	part.	(It is used to attach to the end of a sentence to indicate inference or a rhetorical question)
47.	心眼儿	xīnyǎnr	n.	intelligence; cleverness
48.	结了	jié le		(see note 11)
49.	盛	chéng	v.	fill
50.	扳子	bānzi	n.	wrench
51.	使	shǐ	v.	use; employ
52.	摊儿	tānr	n.	stall; vendor's stand by a road or on a square
53.	哎呀	āiyā	interj.	(expressing surprise or amazement)
54.	差点儿	chà diǎnr		almost
55.	冤枉	yuānwang	v.	accuse (sb) wrongly

王大爷：小伙子，小伙子！

小伙子：什么事，大爷？

王大爷：**上回**你给我二十块钱，我得找你十块钱，我都等你**好**^{N14}**几天**了。

小伙子：哎哟，大爷，不就十块钱吗，您就**搁**您那_儿吧，我这车**保不齐**^{N15}哪天坏了，还上您这_儿修**嘛**。

王大爷：**别价**^{N16}，别价，这一码归一码^{N17}。

小伙子：大爷，您也太**认真**了吧，不就十块钱**嘛**？

王大爷：小伙子，你大爷我这个人啊，**心里**搁不住事_儿^{N18}，把钱还给你了，我这心里就**踏实**了。

56. （上）回	(shàng)huí	m.	last time（same as 上次）
57. 好几天	hǎo jǐ tiān		quite a few days
58. 搁	gē	v.	put；place
59. 保不齐	bǎobuqí	adv.	(see note 15)
60. 嘛	ma	part.	(used to emphasize the obvious)
61. 别价	biéjie	adv.	(see note 16)
62. 认真	rènzhēn	adj.	serious
63. 心里	xīnli		in the heart；in the mind
64. 踏实	tāshi	adj.	feel at ease；steadfast

小伙子：就为十块钱，您**至于**吗^{N19}？

王大爷：**做人**就得**讲信誉**。

65.	至于	zhìyú	v.	there is no need; not necessary
66.	做人	zuò rén	vo.	conduct oneself
67.	讲	jiǎng	v.	pay attention to
68.	信誉	xìnyù	n.	reputation

注释 Notes

1. **"一……都/也十不/没"：**

这个格式的意思是"完全没有……"。比如"我一分钱都没带"意思是"我完全没有带钱"。又如：

This pattern suggests absolute negation. It literally means "not even one...". For instance，"我一分钱都没带" means "I don't even have one penny." See more examples below：

（1）下课了，教室里一个人都没有了。

The class is over，and there is nobody in the classroom.

（2）昨天去商店，我一件衣服都没买。

I went shopping yesterday but didn't buy even one piece of clothing.

（3）这里我一个人都不认识。

I don't know anyone here.

2. **"（今天）是什么日子这是？"：**

这个句子的意思是："今天这是什么日子？"说话人把自己认为重要的话（通常是谓语的主要部分）放在句子开头，把主语以及某些状语放在句末。这种现象叫倒装句或"追加"。有时句末追加的部分也可能在前面出现了，比如上面句子里的"是"。口语里常出现这种句子。再如：

"（今天）是什么日子这是？" "What's the occasion?" In this sentence the verb "是" is placed at the beginning of the sentence, and the subject "这" is put at the end of the sentence. This phenomenon is called "inverted sentence". The speaker usually does this when she/he considers the fronted element，often the predicate，to be more important than the subject. Sometimes the predicate is copied at the end for further emphasis. This kind of structure often occurs in colloquial speech. See more examples below：

（1）去哪儿了你？

Where did you go?

（2）有课吗你明天？

Do you have class tomorrow?

（3）你这是买的什么呀，这是？

My goodness, what did you buy?

3. "解解馋，补补":

这是动词重叠形式。"解馋"的意思是"吃到足够的想吃的东西"。"补"在这里的意思是"补养"，一般中国人认为某些食物或药物可以使身体更健康、更强壮。口语。

"解解馋，补补" is a form of verb duplication. "解馋" means to "satisfy one's appetite", and "补" means "to build up one's health by taking nutritious food". Chinese people generally believe that some particular foods and tonics have special function of nurturing one's body. A colloquial expression.

4. "还是":

表示经过比较后得出的结论。

"还是" suggests a conclusion drawn from comparison.

(1) 还是你知道心疼我。(跟别人比较)

After all, you are the one who cares about me.

(2) A：周末做什么？看书还是看电影？

what are you going to do this weekend? Study or watch movies?

B：还是看书吧，快考试了。

Let's do some reading, since the test is looming.

(3) A：明年我去哪儿学中文好？

Where should I go to study Chinese next year?

B：还是去北京吧。(跟别的城市比)

Better go to Beijing.

5. "一":

"一"在动词前表示一个短暂的动作完成，后边通常紧跟另一个分句或动词短语（常出现在"一……就"的格式中）。

"一……就……" means "as soon as..., then...". This structure indicates that two actions take place in quick succession, i. e., as soon as action 1 or situation 1 takes place, action 2 follows in temporal or logical order.

(1) 你一说这钱，我就想起来了。

Your mentioning money reminded me.

(2) 这一课很容易，我一听就懂了。

This lesson is easy, and I understood it right away.

(3) 那个学校离这儿不远，你往前一走就看到了。

That school is not far from here. You'll see it after a short walk straightforward.

6. **"冒傻气"**:

"冒"是"向外透"的意思，"傻气"形容不聪明、糊涂的样子，"冒傻气"就是"向外透傻气"，用来形容一个人说了"傻话"或做了"傻事"。口语。

"冒傻气"，a colloquial expression，meaning "to look foolish". It is used to describe someone who did something or said something thoughtless, a colloquial expression. For example：

(1) 我说你又冒傻气，都不认识人家就把钱借出去?

I'm telling you，what you did was foolish. How can you lend money to someone you didn't even know?

(2) 我弟弟老冒傻气，别人说什么他都信。

My (younger) brother is often a fool, he believes whatever people say to him.

(3) 你别冒傻气了，没有免费的午餐。

Don't be stupid, there's no such thing as a free lunch.

7. **"都不认识就"**:

这个句子是从"连认识都不认识就……"来的，意思类似"还不认识就……"。

"都不认识就" is a colloquial way to say "连认识都不认识就……"（"you don't even know him and yet you..."）.

8. **"没下文"**:

意思是"（在一件事情之后），没有出现应该出现的消息或结果"。口语。

"没下文"：a colloquial expression, it literally means "no further mention of it". This expression indicates that the desired result or event will not happen, as expected.

(1) 等着瞧吧，肯定没下文了。

Just wait and see, you won't hear anything from him.

这个句子的意思是"你等着看吧，他借了你的钱，以后肯定不会还给你了。"

In this case, the speaker says："Just wait and see, he will not return the money he borrowed, as he promised."

(2) 老张答应帮我找工作，可是他说了以后，就没有下文了。

Lao Zhang promised to find a job for me, but I haven't heard anything from him since.

（3）那个公司说可能会买我们的产品，可是他们打过电话以后就没有下文了。

That company said that they will purchase our products, but I haven't heard anything from them since they last called.

9. "打水漂"：

本来的意思是用薄石片平着打过水面，可以溅起一串浪花，课文中"只当它打水漂了"的意思是"就当做把钱扔到水里去了"。"打水漂了"常比喻钱像扔在水里一样没有了。口语。

"打水漂" means "to skip pebbles across the water". This expression is usually used to refer to money that has been spent for nothing. By using this expression, the speaker means that "the money will not be returned, so we should try our best to forget about it." It is a colloquial expression.

10. "长心眼儿"：

意思是多考虑考虑，变得更聪明。口语。

"长心眼儿"：a colloquial expression that means "to become smarter or more mindful（to keep an eye out for suspicious situations）."

11. "结了"：

"结"是"结束、完"的意思。口语。

"结了"：a colloquial expression that means "to end（something），period".

（1）以后长点儿心眼儿就结了。（也可以说：以后长心眼就得了。）

Learn to be smart later on.

（2）你不要说了，我照你说的做不就结了。

Don't nag anymore, I will just follow what you say, OK?

（3）你书还回去就结了，不会罚钱。

Just return the book. You won't be fined.

12. "不好意思"：

约会迟到，借东西忘了及时还等等，可以说"不好意思"。是客气话，一般不用于亲人之间。

"不好意思" is an expression of politeness. It is often used on such occasions in which one is late for an appointment, or when one has forgotten to return something. It is not usually used among family members.

（1）来晚了，不好意思。

Sorry，I am late.

（2）（打电话）喂，我今天不能去了，不好意思啊。

Sorry, but I can't make it today.

（3）李先生：（张先生和王先生正在交谈）不好意思，我有点儿急事，能不能先问一下张先生？

I'm sorry, but I have something urgent to ask Mr. Zhang about.

13. **口语中可以在句末重复主语"我"，也可以重复"你"（通常出现在问话中）**

   The pronoun "我" or "你" serving as the subject can be repeated at the end of the sentence in a colloquial style. (This phenomenon is often seen in questions)

（1）我忘了我。

I forgot.

（2）你去哪儿了你？我到处找你。

Where have you been? I've been looking for you everywhere.

（3）你怎么哭了你？

Why are you crying?

14. **"好"：**

   副词，强调数量多或时间久。如：好几年、好多人、好久。口语。副词"好"也表示程度高，用在形容词和表示心理活动的动词前。口语。如：好热、好冷、好远、好大。

   "好" as an adverb, often occurs before an adjective or a stative verb to suggest a greater extent of a (psychological) state. It is a colloquial expression. Also see "好热、好冷、好远、好大" etc.

（1）我都等了你好几天了。

I've been waiting for you for quite a few days.

（2）我们好长时间没见面了。

We haven't seen each other for quite a while.

（3）那儿有好多人。

There are quite a few people there.

15. **"保不齐"：**

   意思是"可能"，口语。

   It means "perhaps", a colloquial expression.

（1）你带着伞吧，保不齐会下雨。

You'd better bring an umbrella with you, it will probably rain.

（2）别急，钱包保不齐落在家里了。

Don't panic，your purse might have been left at home.

（3）你再给他打个电话吧，他保不齐忘了。

You should call him again，he may have forgotten.

16. **"别价"**：

也写作"别介"。北方方言，意思同表示劝阻或制止的"别"。口语。

"别价"，also written as "别介"，is a colloquial expression used in the Northern dialect，means "don't...".

17. **"一码归一码"**：

也可以说"一码是一码"。"码"是"事"的量词。"一码归一码"的意思是"这是两件事，要分清楚"。

"码" is the measure word of "事" （"matter"）. "一码归一码" also said as "一码是一码"，means "Here are two separate matters，and they can't make up for each other."

18. **"心里搁不住事儿"**：

"搁"是"放"的意思。"心里"指的是"思想里"。

"心里搁不住事儿"的意思是"老想着某件事（不做或不说出来心里不踏实）"。

"心里" means "in one's heart"，"搁" means "to place". "心里搁不住事儿" literally means "One cannot hide any emotion or secret，and must somehow show it （whether by facial expressions，or by actions）." This expression indicates that one cannot help but worry about things.

19. **"至于吗"**：

"至于"有一个意思是"达到某种程度"。常用"不至于"或反问句，意思是没有达到那种程度。

"至于吗" means "Is it worth it？Isn't that going a bit too far？" This expression is more often used in rhetorical form.

（1）它不就是条狗嘛，你至于吗？哎，你不怕邻居们笑话呀？

All that just for a dog？Aren't you afraid of being laughed at by the neighbors？

这句话的意思是：这只是一条狗，你这么喜欢它，把它看得像人一样，邻居会笑话你。

Here，Nana's husband means："This is a dog，and yet you love it so much you treat it like a human being. You will be a laughingstock among

the neighbors."

（2）就是感冒了，你至于怕成这个样子吗？

It's just a cold, you don't need to be so scared!

（3）这次考试我考得很不好，可是不至于不及格。

I did do bad on the test, but I didn't do badly enough to fail.

听说练习　**Listening & Speaking Exercises**

■ **一、课文理解 Text Comprehension**

（一）根据故事情节选择适当的答案

Please choose the most appropriate answer based on the story

1. 在剧中，小伙子第一次到王大爷这儿来是为了（　　　）

　　A. 借钱　　　　　　　　B. 修车　　　　　　　　C. 借扳子

2. 小伙子把什么东西忘在家里了？（　　　）

　　A. 钥匙　　　　　　　　B. 钱包　　　　　　　　C. 钥匙和钱包

3. 小伙子说他什么时候会再来？（　　　）

　　A. 今天下班以后

　　B. 明天上班以前

　　C. 今天下午

4. 王大爷的老伴儿给他做红烧排骨是因为（　　　）

　　A. 那天是一个好日子

　　B. 她觉得王大爷身体不好

　　C. 她觉得王大爷工作很辛苦

5. 王大爷的老伴儿认为小伙子（　　　）

　　A. 认识王大爷

　　B. 麻烦王大爷

　　C. 骗王大爷

6. 王大爷的老伴儿（　　　）

　　A. 很在乎钱

　　B. 很在乎王大爷的身体

　　C. 很在乎王大爷的工作

7. 小伙子又来到王大爷修车的地方是因为他想（　　　）

　　A. 借钱　　　　　　　　B. 修车　　　　　　　　C. 借扳子

8. 小伙子给了王大爷（　　　）

    A. 十块钱 　　　　　　　B. 二十块钱 　　　　　　C. 三十块钱

9. 王大爷着急把钱还给小伙子因为他觉得（　　　）

    A. 钱最重要

    B. 信誉最重要

    C. 修车最重要

（二）根据课文判断下面句子意思的正误

State whether the following statements are true or false based on the story

1. （　　　）小伙子以前认识王大爷。

2. （　　　）小伙子修车的时候发现他忘了带钱了。

3. （　　　）王大爷不想借给小伙子钱。

4. （　　　）王大爷的老伴觉得小伙子肯定不会还钱。

5. （　　　）王大爷觉得他挣钱挣得比较容易。

6. （　　　）小伙子给了王大爷二十块钱，因为他觉得有一点儿不好意思。

7. （　　　）王大爷一直在等着小伙子，因为要找给他十块钱。

8. （　　　）王大爷觉得他给别人一个什么样的印象比钱更重要。

（三）先听故事叙述，然后复述故事

Listen to the narrative first and then retell the story

    早上王大爷修车的时候，一个小伙子过来跟他借十块钱，因为他着急上班，把钱包和钥匙都锁在家里了。王大爷借给了他十块钱。王大爷的老伴儿知道这件事以后，觉得王大爷肯定受骗了，以后再有这样的事得长点儿心眼儿。几天过去了，小伙子真的没有把钱还给王大爷。

    但是，这个小伙子不是骗子，只是把这件事忘了。后来王大爷又见到他，说到那十块钱的时候，小伙子觉得很不好意思。他给了王大爷二十块钱，因为他们都没有十块钱。

    王大爷等了小伙子好几天，才见到他。王大爷还给了小伙子十块钱。在王大爷看来，人的信誉最重要。

二、词语使用 Application of Vocabulary and Grammar

（一）选择题

Choose the item that is grammatically correct

1. 我这个周末不能出去，因为明天有一个考试，可是我还一点儿_____没复习呢。

A. 只　　　　　　　　B. 就　　　　　　　　C. 都

2. 昨天我要去上课的时候发现我的车坏了，没有办法，只能＿＿＿＿＿＿＿＿＿朋友借了一辆自行车。

A. 给　　　　　　　　B. 管　　　　　　　　C. 从

3. 他早上看见王大爷在那儿修车，才想＿＿＿＿＿＿＿＿＿忘了给王大爷带钱了。

A. 起来　　　　　　　B. 上　　　　　　　　C. 着

4. 王大爷的老伴儿认为那个小伙子借了十块钱以后＿＿＿＿＿＿＿＿＿不还了。

A. 肯定　　　　　　　B. 决定　　　　　　　C. 担心

5. 他说回国以后就给我写信，可是一回去就没有＿＿＿＿＿＿＿＿＿了。

A. 写信　　　　　　　B. 打电话　　　　　　C. 下文

（二）选择题

Circle the answer that best reflects the meaning of the sentence

1. 我就借十块钱，下了班我就给您还回来。（　　　）

A. 我现在就借钱

B. 我就要借钱了

C. 我只借十块钱

D. 我已经借了十块钱了

2. 我这车都在您这儿修的。（　　　）

A. 每次我的车坏了都是在您这儿修的

B. 我有很多车，都是您修的

C. 我的车都要在您这儿修

D. 我的车都修好了

3. 他拿了你的钱，肯定没下文了。（　　　）

A. 他把你的钱借走了，以后一定不会把钱还给你的

B. 他一定用你的钱买东西了

C. 他把你的钱借走了，以后也不会给你写信

D. 他把你的钱借走了，可能忘了还给你

4. 不就十块钱吗？只当它打水漂了。（　　　）

A. 十块钱不够，你应该多给他几块

B. 你只有十块钱，为什么要借给他？

C. 只是十块钱，算了吧，别再想了

D. 他会把那十块钱丢在水里

5. 以后长点_儿心眼_儿就结了。（　　）

A. 以后你最好别借给别人钱

B. 以后你跟别人打交道的时候小心一点_儿就行了

C. 以后你不能跟他打交道了

D. 以后你不要随便相信小伙子

6. 我这车保不齐哪天坏了，还上您这_儿修。（　　）

A. 我的车以后可能还会坏，如果坏了，我还要来您这_儿修

B. 我的车那天坏了，我还来找您修过车

C. 万一我的车坏了，我还来找您修

D. 想不到我的车那天坏了，我来找您修过车

7. 我这个人心里搁不住事_儿。（　　）

A. 我总是着急

B. 如果发生了什么事情，我会总想着它

C. 我不喜欢跟别人借钱

D. 我很关心别人的事情

8. 就为十块钱，您至于吗？（　　）

A. 您只给我十块钱，为什么？

B. 为了十块钱，您有一点_儿认真

C. 您不应该给我十块钱

D. 只为了十块钱，您不应该这样

（三）选择适当的词语，替换句中的画线部分

Choose the most appropriate words to replace the underlined parts

A. 一 MW（N）都……	B. 不就结了	C. 保不齐
D. 是冒傻气	E. 心里搁不住事_儿	F. 想不起来
G. 解解搀	H. 就没有下文了	

1. 我的同屋很有意思，不管谁管他借钱他都借。有的人觉得他这样做<u>不聪明</u>，但是我不这样想。

2. 今天早上我妈妈给我打电话问我什么时候回家，她说要给我做我最爱吃的红烧牛肉，让我好好<u>美餐一顿</u>。

3. A：真糟糕！我下了课就跟朋友去打篮球，忘了给女朋友打电话了！

B：没关系，现在给她打个电话解释一下就可以了。

4. A：不管是在美国还是在中国，名牌大学的毕业生一般都能找到好工作。

   B：我觉得名牌大学的学生可能也找不到好工作。

5. 春天开学的时候，她说放假以后我们一起开车出去玩儿，可是一放假她就上暑期学校了，出去玩儿的事儿她就没有再说。

6. A：要是你总是觉得不舒服，应该给你妈妈打个电话。

   B：不行，我妈妈有一点儿小事就老想着。我不能让她为我担心。

7. A：对不起，我忘了在哪儿见过你了。

   B：我们不是邻居吗？我家就在你住的那座红楼后边。

8. A：哎，我只有一张十块钱，你有没有两张五块的？我想换一下。

   B：我现在身上没有钱。

（四）用所给词语完成对话

Complete the following dialogues with the items provided in the parenthesis

1.（想起来了，不好意思）

   A：小李，我现在要用我的自行车。

   B：你的自行车？

   A：你昨天不是借我的自行车了吗？

   B：我_____，_____，现在就还给你。

2.（肯定，一……就……）

   A：我们吃了晚饭再去看七点的电影还来得及吗？

   B：_____来得及，我们_____吃完饭_____走。

3.（好几 MW N 了，还是 VV）

   A：周末我们一起吃顿中国饭吧！

   B：这个星期我吃了_____，我们_____日本饭吧。

4.（想起来了，肯定）

   A：我怎么找不到我的车钥匙了？

   B：你刚才穿的不是这件衣服吧？

   A：我_____，_____是在那件衣服兜里。

（五）角色扮演 Role play

Make a dialogue with a classmate. One party plays Uncle Wang, and the other plays the young man. Your dialogue should incorporate the provided items.

小伙子	王大爷
You just found that you left your wallet at home，but you don't have time to go back since you are already late for work. At this moment you spot Uncle Wang, the bike repairer who sits at the corner of the street fixing bikes for people everyday. How about you borrow 10 *yuan* from him for lunch today, and return it to him tomorrow?	You are a little surprised when this young man tries to borrow 10 *yuan* from you. He looks sincere and anxious, so you agree to lend him 10 *yuan*. However, you want to remind him to return the money to you—because it is not easy for you to earn 10 *yuan*.
1. 把……锁在家里了 2. 一 MW（N）都没 V 3. 借 4. 还回来	1. 管……借钱？ 2. 够 3. 忘了 4. 不那么容易

三、课堂讨论 Discussion

1. 如果你是王大爷，你会做同样的事情吗（把钱借给别人以后又提醒别人还钱）？为什么？
2. 王大爷是不是太认真了？
3. 如果一个朋友借了一本你最喜欢的书，一直没有还给你，你会怎么办？
4. 周末到了，你的朋友想跟你借五十块钱，他说下星期会还给你，你借不借给他？为什么？

第三课 今天，属于妈妈

Today Belongs to Mother

编剧：张雁

人物 (Characters)

母亲 （mǔqin）——守寡多年的母亲。

小美 （Xiǎoměi）——女儿，高校研究生。

赵叔 （Zhào shū）——母亲的同事。

大军 （Dàjūn）——女儿第一次登门的男朋友。

---

1. 属于	shǔyú	v.	belong to
2. 母亲	mǔqin	n.	mother
3. 守寡	shǒu guǎ	vo.	live in widowhood
4. 高校	gāoxiào	n.	college；university
5. 赵叔/	Zhào shū/	N.	Uncle Zhao
赵叔叔	Zhào shūshū		
6. 同事	tóngshì	n.	colleague；co-worker；workmate
7. 登门	dēng mén	vo.	pay a visit to someone's house

课 文 Text

大　军：哎哟，你看我这大包小包的[N1]，哎哟，你走那么快干吗[N2]呀？

小　美：干什么呀？我都快一年多没见着我妈了，就这①，我还觉着慢呢。

小　美：这还差不多，我可[N3]告诉你啊，我妈就我这么一个宝贝闺女，你要是连她这第一关都[N4]过不了的话，咱俩的事，可就哪儿说哪儿了[N5]了啊。

大　军：你别吓唬我，我可胆小[N6]。

小　美：你放心吧，我喜欢的我妈还能不喜欢哪！不过，咱们可得把话先说清楚了，我妈她一人过了十几年，也怪不容易的，以后我到哪儿，我妈就得到哪儿。

8. 包	bāo	n.	bag
9. 干吗	gànmá	pron.	why; what for
10. 干什么	gàn shénme		why; what to do
11. 觉着	juézhe	v.	feel
12. 宝贝	bǎobèi	n.	treasure
13. 闺女	guīnü	n.	daughter
14. 过不了	guò bu liǎo	vc.	unable to pass
15. 咱俩	zán liǎ	pron.	two of us
16. 吓唬	xiàhu	v.	frighten; scare
17. 胆小	dǎn xiǎo		timid
18. 放心	fàng xīn	vo.	rest assured; not to worry
19. 怪	guài	adv.	very; quite

① "这"的意思是"这样"。

大　军：哎呀……

小　美：要是咱们真**结了婚**，我妈可得跟我住。

大　军：我当然是没问题了，那就不知道她**老人家**是不是愿意跟咱们一起住嘛，她**万一**要是……

小　美：那是我妈，我还能不知道？

大　军：哎……

小　美：**好了**，大军，就到这儿吧，我觉着还是应该先跟我妈先说一下，要不**搞**得咱们**像先斩后奏**N7**似的**。你呀，到那边的**花园**先去**待会**儿，等我给你**信**儿N8，啊！

大　军：那好，你可**麻利**点儿啊，这要是让我等时间长了，我可**冲**进去了。

小　美：你**敢**！

小　美：妈。

母　亲：小美？你怎么回来啦？也不**事先**给妈**捎**个话N9。

20.	结(了)婚	jié (le) hūn	vo.	get married
21.	老人家	lǎorénjiā	n.	(an respectful form of address for an old person)
22.	万一	wànyī	adv.	in case
23.	好了	hǎo le		OK；that's enough
24.	搞	gǎo	v.	make
25.	像…似的	xiàng…shìde		be like…
26.	先斩后奏	xiān zhǎn hòu zòu		(see note 7)
27.	花园	huāyuán	n.	garden
28.	待会儿	dāihuìr		stay for a moment；wait a moment
29.	信儿	xìnr	n.	message
30.	麻利	máli	adj.	quick
31.	冲	chōng	v.	dash；stride
32.	敢	gǎn	modal.	dare
33.	事先	shìxiān	t.	in advance；beforehand
34.	捎	shāo	v.	send (a message)

小　美：想给你一个**惊喜**呀。哎，妈，你今儿怎么这么**年轻**啊？
母　亲：**哪儿有的事**啊，你这孩子**净**瞎说。

小　美：哎，我说，妈，你怎么知道今儿我要回来呀？
母　亲：妈去给你买**西瓜**啊……
小　美：妈，妈，别累着，我有话跟你说，来。
母　亲：妈不累。
小　美：谁呀？
母　亲：我来我来，可能是找我的。

陌生人：哎，请问王**处长**在家吗？
母　亲：您**找错**了，对面。
陌生人：哦，哦，对不起，对不起。
母　亲：咳，**找错门**了。
小　美：妈，你坐，我有话跟你说。
母　亲：别忙，妈那儿还有个汤没做呢，啊。
小　美：谁呀？

35. 惊喜	jīngxǐ	n.	pleasant surprise
36. 年轻	niánqīng	adj.	young
37. 哪儿有的事	nǎr yǒu de shì		that's nonsense
38. 净	jìng	adv.	purely; completely
39. 西瓜	xīguā	n.	watermelon
40. 陌生人	mòshēng rén	n.	stranger
41. 处长	chùzhǎng	n.	head of a department or office; section chief
42. 找错	zhǎo cuò	vc.	look for (somebody or something) at a wrong place; arrive at a wrong place
43. 找错门	zhǎo cuò mén		come to a wrong door

赵　叔：小美!?

小　美：赵叔!? 您够^{N10}**浪漫**的呀，这是?……

赵　叔：这两天呀，你妈有点儿不舒服……我**代表工会**把这个……
　　　　送给她。

小　美：妈你怎么啦?

母　亲：没事了，一点儿**小病**，头疼**脑**热的**不要紧**。

小　美：赵叔，您呀，还^{N11}真有**情调**。

小　美：我进去接个电话啊。

母　亲：哎，一会儿你跟她说。

赵　叔：你跟她说。

母　亲：还是你跟她说。

44.	浪漫	làngmàn	adj.	romantic; unconventional
45.	代表	dàibiǎo	v.	represent; be on behalf of
46.	工会	gōnghuì	n.	labor union; trade union
47.	脑	nǎo	n.	brain; head
48.	不要紧	bù yàojǐn		It doesn't matter
49.	情调	qíngdiào	n.	sentiment; taste

小　美：妈。

母　亲：哎。

母　亲：呃，我去盛汤啊。

小　美：赵叔，来。

赵　叔：哎，哎。小美，赵叔想跟你说个事。

小　美：**嗯**，您说。

赵　叔：是这么个事，我……咳，我就直说了吧，我跟你妈，我们俩想**领个证**[N12]，以后呢，就在一起生活。你看……你的**意见**？

小　美：不是……您，说您……和我妈她……

赵　叔：对，就是这个意思，我跟你妈**考虑**好久了。**本来**想早点儿告诉你，可你妈老是**犹犹豫豫**的。

小　美：妈，妈。这天大的好事啊这是！

小　美：大军，对不起，咱们的事还是明天再说吧。我**一直**都以为我是妈妈的**全部**，但我忘了，妈妈也应该有她自己的**幸福**呀，我真是太**自私**了。今天是个**好日子**——但应该属于妈妈……

50. 嗯	ń	interj.	（an exclamation)
51. 领（个)证	lǐng (ge) zhèng	vo.	apply the certificate; receive the certificate
52. 意见	yì·jiàn	n.	view; opinion
53. 考虑	kǎolù	v.	consider; think about
54. 本来	běnlái	adv.	originally; at first
55. 犹犹豫豫	yóu yóu yù yù	adj.	hesitant
56. 一直	yìzhí	adv.	always; all along
57. 全部	quánbù		totality; entirety
58. 幸福	xìngfú	adj./n.	happy; happiness
59. 自私	zìsī	adj.	selfish; self-centered
60. 好日子	hǎo rìzi		auspicious date; happy occasion

1. **"……的"**：

句末用"的"有描写作用。例如：

"的" at the end of a sentence often serves a descriptive function，e. g. ：

(1) 你看我这大包小包的。（意思是：你看我这拿着大包小包的样子。）

Look at me carrying so many bags of all sizes.

(2) 别慢慢吞吞的了。

Don't be so slow and languid!

(3) 我本来想早点儿告诉你，可你妈老犹犹豫豫的。

I would have told you earlier，but your mom was always hesitant.

2. **"干吗"**：

同"干什么"，意思是"做什么"。也可以问原因，包含有点儿奇怪的语气。口语。

"干吗" like "干什么"，often means simply "what to do". As a colloquialism，it can also be used to ask about the reason for something，often carrying a tone of being surprised.

(1) 你走那么快干吗呀？

Why are you walking so fast?

(2) 他干吗跟你生气？

Why was he angry at you?

(3) 今天的电影很好看，你干吗不去？

Today's movie was really good. How come you didn't go?

3. **副词"可"（一）**：

副词"可"在口语里可以加强语气，有时含有"出乎意料"的意思。可以用于陈述句、祈使句和感叹句。

Adverb 可（I）：In spoken Chinese，the adverb "可" can strengthen the tone in a statement，an imperative or exclamatory sentence. Sometimes it suggests that something is out of the listener's reckoning.

(1) 我可告诉你啊，我妈就我这么一个宝贝闺女，……

Let me tell you, I'm my mom's only darling daughter...

（2）你要是连她这一关都过不了的话，咱俩的事，可就哪儿说哪儿了了。

If you can't even pass her, the relationship between us will end where it has started.

（3）你别吓唬我，我可胆小。

Don't try to scare me. I'm a timid person.

（4）咱们可得把话说清楚了，……

Let's get everything clear between us...

（5）你可麻利点儿，这要是让我等时间长了，我可冲进去了。

Try to be quick! If you make me wait too long, I will just dash in.

4. "连……都/也"：

这个格式的作用是：在同类事物或同类情况中，提出一个极端的情况（如最好的、最坏的，最大的、最小的，最高的、最低的等），后边的句子表示由这个情况得出的结论：其他同类事物也不例外。

The structure "连……都/也" highlights an extreme example of all things or situations of the same type, e. g. , the best/the worst, the biggest/the smallest, the tallest/the lowest, etc. It suggests that, if the extreme example leads to a certain conclusion, all other things or situations of the same type will be no exceptions.

（1）A：那个小孩儿跑得快吗？

Does that child run fast?

B：她连走都不会呢。

She can't even walk.

B的意思是：一个孩子要会跑，先得会走。"她"不会走，当然不可能跑得快。

What B suggests is that one needs to be able to walk before becoming able to run. If the child can't even walk, of course she can't run fast.

（2）这个人我连他的名字都不知道，怎么会认识他呢？

I don't even know his name. How can I be his acquaintance?

（3）我姐姐会说很多外语，连阿拉伯语都会。（说话人认为在外语中，阿拉伯语是最难、会说的人很少的。）

My older sister speaks several foreign languages, even Arabic. (The speaker considers Arab one of the most difficult languages.)

（4）我可告诉你啊，我妈就我这么一个宝贝闺女，你要是连她这一关都过不了的话，咱俩的事，可就哪儿说哪儿了了。

Let me tell you：I'm my mom's only darling daughter，if you can't even pass her，the relationship between us will end where it has started.

例（4）在本剧中的意思是：因为妈妈只有"我"一个女儿，所以她的意见最重要，"她这一关"也是最先要过的。如果她不同意"我们"的事，那"我们"的事就完了。

In our play，this sentence suggests：Since I am my mother's only daughter，her opinions are most important，and our relationship has to be endorsed by her before anyone else. If you fail to win her endorsement，it will be the end to our relationship.

5. "哪儿说哪儿了"：

字面意思是"在哪儿说的话，就在哪儿算完了"。通常表示"（我们）说的话不要告诉别人，不要让别人知道"。

The expression "哪儿说哪儿了" literally means "The words will be finished where they are said." It often serves as a proposal to keep what is said as a secret and not to divulge it to others，e. g. ：

这件事我就告诉你了，咱们哪儿说哪儿了，千万别告诉别人。

I have only told this to you. Let's keep it between us，and never tell it to anyone else.

本剧中"你要是连她这一关都过不了的话，咱俩的事，可就哪儿说哪儿了了"，意思是：他俩的事就没有"以后/将来"了，就结束了。

In this play，however，the sentence——"咱俩的事，可就哪儿说哪儿了了" means：There will be the end to our relationship.

6. "你别吓唬我，我可胆小"：

当预料对方会说出自己怕听到的事情时，可以这样说。

The expression "你别吓唬我，我可胆小" can be used when one anticipates that what the other person says will be scary.

7. "先斩后奏"：

"斩"的意思是"杀（罪犯）"，"奏"的意思是"臣子向皇帝报告"。"先斩后奏"的意思是：事情先做了，然后再向有关的人报告或说明。

"先斩后奏"：The verb "斩" means "to execute (a criminal)"，and the verb "奏" means "to memorialize the ruler (by a subject)". The set phrase "先斩后奏" thus means doing something without seeking the approval or informing the relevant parties first.

(1) 我觉着还是应该跟我妈先说一下，要不搞得咱们像先斩后奏似的。

I think we should talk to my mom first. Otherwise it would be like executing the criminal without memorializing the emperor first.

这句话的意思是："……要不然（如果不先跟我妈说）咱们好像先确定了关系才跟她说一样。"

What is suggested here is that, if we don't talk to my mother first, it would seem that we have certified our relationship even before she gets to know it.

(2) 公司的大事你不能先斩后奏。

In regard to the important matters in the company, you are not supposed to execute the criminal without memorializing the emperor first.

(3) 房子已经买了你才来问我同意不同意，你这样先斩后奏，我不给你钱！

You came to ask for my opinions only after you had already bought the house! Since you executed the criminal before memorializing the emperor, I have no money for you.

8. **"等我给你信儿"**:

"信儿"的意思是"消息"。口语。

"等我给你信儿"：Here "信儿" is a colloquial word for "message", not necessarily a "letter".

9. **"捎个话"**:

"捎个话"本来的意思是"请别人带话给某人"。这里的意思是事先告诉一下。

"捎个话"：It literally means "to ask someone to pass on a message to a third party". In the context of the play it means to inform someone in advance.

10. **"够"**:

意思是达到某种程度。

"够" followed by an adjective, means reaching a substantial extent.

(1) 哟，是赵叔，您够浪漫的呀。

Oh, it's Uncle Zhao! You're truly romantic.

(2) 这件衣服够好的了，你就买了吧。

This shirt is really nice. Why don't you buy it?

(3) 那个地方可够冷的，你别去了。

It's really cold in that place. Don't go there.

（4）这儿这么多人，够热闹的！

There are so many people here. It's really bustling!

（5）今天的考试够难的。

Today's exam was very difficult.

11. "还"（一）：

表示"没有想到"，有赞叹的语气。（又见第四课注释10）

"还"（I）: It can suggest the speaker's slight surprise at something that has taken place, often in an approving tone (also see note 10 in Lesson 4).

（1）赵叔，您呀，还真有情调。

Uncle Zhao, you are not without some romantic sentiments.

（2）你正在考试，我以为你不能来了，想不到你还真来了。

You were taking the exam, and I thought you wouldn't come. Who would have expected you to be here?

（3）你还真有办法，这么难请的人你都请来了。

You are indeed resourceful. Those people seldom accept invitations, and you got them here!

12. "我们想领个证"：

意思是我们想领结婚证，想结婚。

"我们想领个证"：Here "证" refers to the marriage certificate. "领个证" simply means to apply for the marriage certificate, i. e., to get married.

听说练习　Listening & Speaking Exercises

■ 一、课文理解 Text Comprehension

（一）根据故事情节选择适当的答案

Please choose the most appropriate answer based on the story

1. 大军和小美要去看（　　）

   A. 王处长　　　　　　B. 小美的妈妈　　　　　C. 赵叔

2. 小美的妈妈一人生活了（　　）

   A. 几十年了　　　　　B. 一年多了　　　　　　C. 十几年了

3. 小美看到妈妈时觉得她看起来（　　）

   A. 年轻了　　　　　　B. 很累　　　　　　　　C. 很忙

4. 小美去看妈妈，但是事先没告诉妈妈，是为了给她一个（　　）

   A. 宝贝　　　　　　　B. 惊喜　　　　　　　　C. 礼物

5. 赵叔说拿来的花是（　　）

   A. 工会送给妈妈的

   B. 他送给妈妈的

   C. 他送给小美的

6. 小美没想到母亲（　　）

   A. 知道她回来

   B. 知道他有男朋友了

   C. 会想再结婚

（二）根据课文判断下面句子意思的正误

State whether the following statements are true or false based on the story

1.（　　）大军和小美买了很多东西去看小美的妈妈。

2.（　　）要是小美的妈妈不喜欢大军，小美就不跟大军结婚。

3.（　　）大军不希望小美的妈妈以后跟他们一起住。

4.（　　）妈妈知道今天小美要回来，所以做了很多菜。

5.（   ）小美跟赵叔以前就认识。

6.（   ）小美的母亲今天身体不舒服。

7.（   ）赵叔今天来是为了告诉小美他跟小美妈要结婚了。

8.（   ）大军今天见到了小美的妈妈。

（三）先听故事叙述，然后复述故事

Listen to the narrative first and then retell the story

　　小美有一年多没见着母亲了。今天要去看她，并把她的男朋友大军带来让她看看。因为父亲十几年前就去世了，妈妈一直一个人生活，小美告诉大军他们结婚以后她的母亲要跟他们一起住。

　　为了给妈妈一个惊喜，小美事先没告诉妈妈她要回来。但是妈妈做了很多菜，好像知道他们要来。吃饭前，赵叔来了，还带来了很多花，说是因为妈妈有点儿不舒服，是工会买了花托他送来的。

　　吃饭的时候赵叔说了实话：他和小美妈妈要结婚了。小美听了以后非常高兴，决定先不说自己和大军的事情，因为她觉得今天这个好日子更应该属于妈妈。

二、词语使用 Application of Vocabulary and Grammar

（一）选择题

Choose the item that is grammatically correct

1. 我可告诉你啊，我妈_____我这么一个宝贝闺女，你得先过她这一关。

   A. 爱　　　　　　　　B. 就　　　　　　　　C. 生

2. 我觉着还是应该跟我妈_____说一下，要不搞得咱们像先斩后奏似的。

   A. 先　　　　　　　　B. 得　　　　　　　　C. 要

3. 我妈她一人过_____十几年，也怪不容易的。要是咱们真结了婚，我妈可得跟我住。

   A. 得　　　　　　　　B. 了　　　　　　　　C. 着

4. 哪儿有的事啊，你这孩子_____瞎说。

   A. 净　　　　　　　　B. 能　　　　　　　　C. 会

5. 哦，对不起，对不起。我找_____门了。

   A. 到　　　　　　　　B. 上　　　　　　　　C. 错

6. 我一直_____他是北方人，原来他是从上海来的，北京话说得倍儿棒。

    A. 以为   B. 想   C. 认为

（二）选择题

Circle the answer that best reflects the meaning of the underlined portion of the sentence

1. 我都快一年多没见着我妈了，<u>就这</u>，我还觉着慢呢。（   ）

    A. 就是走这么快

    B. 就没有办法

    C. 就你这么说

    D. 就在这儿

2. 哟，是赵叔!? 您<u>够浪漫的</u>呀，这是? ……（   ）

    A. 浪漫够了

    B. 真浪漫

    C. 可以浪漫

    D. 已经浪漫了

3. 哪有的事啊，你这孩子净<u>瞎说</u>。（   ）

    A. 说不清楚

    B. 说谎

    C. 说错

    D. 乱说

4. 你要是过不了我妈这第一关，咱俩的事，可就<u>哪儿说哪儿</u>了了啊。

                                              （   ）

    A. 不成了

    B. 得多说了

    C. 找地方说

    D. 去哪儿说

5. <u>没事了</u>，一点儿小病，头疼脑热的不要紧……（   ）

    A. 没发生事情

    B. 没病

    C. 事情做完了

    D. 事情解决了（病好了）

6. 你呀，到那边的花园先去待会儿，<u>等我给你信儿</u>啊!（   ）

A. 等我的电话

B. 等我写的信

C. 等我来

D. 等我的消息

7. 你可麻利点儿啊，这要是让我等时间长了，我可冲进去了。（　　　）

A. 别太麻烦

B. 流利一点儿

C. 快一点儿

D. 麻烦点儿

（三）选择适当的词语，替换句中的画线部分

Choose the most appropriate words to replace the underlined parts

A. 可　　　B. 都　　　C. 还　　　D. 犹犹豫豫　　　E. 万一　　　F. 干吗

1. 小军<u>已经</u>要结婚了，她父母还没见过他的女朋友呢。

2. 他早就已经不爱你了，你<u>为什么</u>还老是忘不了他呢？

3. 你最近这么忙，我以为你不能来了，想不到你<u>倒</u>真来了。

4. 最好别开别人的车，<u>要是</u>出了事情，不好办。

5. 王处长，这件事情怎么办你得马上决定，不能老这么<u>想来想去</u>的。

6. 他的话<u>一定</u>不要全信，他爱瞎说。

（四）用所给词语完成对话

Complete the following dialogues with the items provided in the parenthesis

1.（想来想去，看来）

甲：明天小美要回来，是吗？

乙：是。＿＿＿＿＿＿我们的事情应该让她知道了。哎，老赵，明天你把我们的事跟小美说了吧。

甲：可以。但是我＿＿＿＿＿＿觉得还是你跟他说比较好。

乙：还是你跟她说吧。

2.（老犹犹豫豫的，没想到）

甲：小美，我跟你妈要结婚了！

乙：是吗，我真＿＿＿＿＿＿！你为什么一直没告诉我呢？

甲：我本来想早点儿告诉你，可你妈＿＿＿＿＿＿。

3.（哪儿说哪儿了，不就行了）

甲：大军，你一定要让我妈喜欢你，要不然我就不能跟你结婚。

乙：是吗？你喜欢＿＿＿＿＿＿吗？

甲：不行，要是我妈不同意，咱俩的事可就_____。

乙：真的？

4.（对……有……，连……都……）

甲：想什么呢，小赵？

乙：不知你能不能帮忙。我_____那个新来的女孩儿很_____兴趣，你能把她介绍给我吗？

甲：这个人我_____她的名字_____不知道，怎么能给你介绍呢？

乙：你知道谁认识她吗？

5.（干吗，先斩后奏）

甲：爸，我想跟您借点儿钱。

乙：_____？

甲：不知你同意不同意，我刚买了个房子。

乙：房子已经买了你才来问我同意不同意，你这样_____，我不给你钱！

（五）角色扮演 Role play

Make a dialogue with a classmate. One party plays Xiaomei, and the other plays Dajun. Your dialogue should incorporate the provided items.

大军	小美
You're making a trip with your girlfriend, Xiaomei, to visit her mother. It is also the first meeting between you and your mother-in-law. Xiaomei is very excited about this trip. She is also rather anxious to see her mother and is a little concerned about introducing you to her. She wants you to know how important that her mother likes you and the possibility that her mother will live with you after you get married.	You're on your way to visit your mother whom you haven't seen for well over a year. You're also bringing your boyfriend to meet her for the first time. You are anxious to see her and excited about this trip. You want Dajun to know how important that your mother likes him and the possibility that she will live with you after you get married.
1. 大包小包的 2. 干吗 3. 你别…… 4. 我可胆小 5. 当然是没问题了 6. 万一 7. 你可麻利点儿啊	1. 都快一年多了 2. 我可告诉你啊 3. 连……都…… 4. 哪儿说哪儿了 5. 怪不容易的 6. 像……似的

■ 三、课堂讨论 Discussion

1. 小美告诉大军，她妈妈对大军的看法非常重要，要是妈妈不喜欢大军，她是不会跟大军结婚的。你对她这样说有什么看法？

2. 要是你是大军，你愿意跟你太太的父母一起住吗？为什么？

3. 小美为什么没跟她妈妈谈他和大军的事情？

4. 小美为什么说"今天属于妈妈"？

第四课 认 错

Admitting Mistakes

编剧：江伟

人物 （Characters）

圆圆 （Yuányuan）——女，小学生。

妈妈 （māma）

爸爸 （bàba）

韩老师 （Hán lǎoshī）

同学们 （tóngxuémen）

课 文 Text

妈　妈：哎，圆圆，你再好好想想，咱们还**缺**什么？这一出门呀，可得好几天呐。

圆　圆：我呀，什么也不缺，就[N1]缺钱，拿来吧。

妈　妈：不就是**夏令营**吗?[N2]这出门呀，又[N3]不是出国，你要那么多钱干什么呀？

---

1. 认错	rèn cuò	vo.	admit a mistake；apologize
2. 缺	quē	v.	be short of；lack
3. 夏令营	xiàlìngyíng	n.	summer camp

圆　圆：**小气劲**ₙ[N4]的，我这不是跟你逗着玩儿呢嘛，我有钱。

爸　爸：刘季啊。

妈　妈：哟，这是怎么了这是？

爸　爸：这真是怪了，我**明明**记得把钱放在**抽屉**里了，不见了。

妈　妈：就你这脑子啊，**指不定**放在哪儿了呢。

爸　爸：我跟你说啊，**绝对保证**我就放在抽屉里了。

妈　妈：你还绝对呢[N5]，我太**了解**你了……

爸　爸：哎，会不会是圆圆拿的？

妈　妈：哎，你可别瞎**怀疑**孩子啊！

爸　爸：我可没瞎怀疑啊，哎，刚才你没听圆圆说她有钱了吗？她哪儿来的钱哪？

妈　妈：那[N6]她有钱也不一定是你那钱呐。

爸　爸：这就[N7]怪了，你说咱们家三口人，我找圆圆问问去。

爸　爸：圆圆，爸爸有事要问你。

圆　圆：什么事你快问吧，我**该**走了。

爸　爸：你看见爸爸抽屉里的钱了吗？

圆　圆：什么钱？我没看见呀。

爸　爸：来，坐下。圆圆，爸爸昨天可看见你**翻**爸爸的抽屉啦！

4. 小气劲儿	xiǎoqi jìnr		stingy；miserly
5. 明明	míngmíng	adv.	obviously；simply
6. 抽屉	chōuti	n.	drawer
7. 指不定	zhǐbudìng	adv.	perhaps；maybe
8. 绝对	juéduì	adv.	absolutely
9. 保证	bǎozhèng	v.	guarantee；promise
10. 了解	liǎojiě	v.	understand；know（sb）well
11. 怀疑	huáiyí	v.	suspect；doubt
12. 该	gāi	adv.	ought to；should
13. 翻	fān	v.	turn over；turn up

圆　圆：对呀，没错，我找我的日记本来着[N8]，可是没看见有什么[N9]钱呀。

爸　爸：圆圆，爸爸知道你去夏令营要花钱，可是花钱要跟爸爸妈妈要嘛，不能自己去拿呀，你说呢。

圆　圆：爸爸，我**发誓**，我真的没拿。

爸　爸：你给我坐下！你真的没拿，啊！我告诉你，如果爸爸要是**发现**是你拿的话，我告诉你……

妈　妈：哎哎哎，这事情还没有搞清楚呢，你怎么能瞎怀疑孩子呢。

爸　爸：你**甭**管，圆圆，刚才我可听你说你有钱的，你哪儿来的钱呐？啊！

圆　圆：爸爸，你还[N10]真怀疑我**偷**你的钱啦？那是我**姥姥**给的，跟你没关系！

妈　妈：哎，圆圆！

同学1：哟，圆圆，你来啦。

同学2：圆圆，快上车呀。

同学3：圆圆，快坐我这儿吧。

妈　妈：你看看，这，她连吃的东西都没有带[N11]，我得给她**送过去**。

14.	发誓	fā shì	vo.	swear; vow
15.	发现	fāxiàn	v.	find out
16.	甭	béng	adv.	need not; no need to
17.	偷	tōu	v.	steal
18.	姥姥	lǎolao	n.	(maternal) grandmother
19.	送过去	sòng guoqu	vc.	deliver/carry (something over)

爸　　爸：唉，找到了，找到了，找到了。你瞧瞧我这**记性**，放在这兜里面了。

妈　　妈：找着了？

爸　　爸：找到了，**刚好**。

妈　　妈：那圆圆怎么办？她可是**赌气**走的啊。

爸　　爸：小孩子嘛……她一会儿就好了。哎，要不等她回来，我请她吃肯德基？

妈　　妈：你说得倒[N12]轻巧，这孩子一走就是好几天，这几天她怎么**熬**啊？我看呀，你得为这事向她**道歉**。

爸　　爸：哪儿有**老子**给孩子道歉的？一点儿面子都没有嘛，我不去。

妈　　妈：你去不去？

妈　　妈：他这个人呀，死[N13]**要面子**，让他跟圆圆**开口**道歉，他**死活**[N14]都说不出口。

爸　　爸：这点儿**小事有必要**嘛？

20.	记性	jìxing	n.	memory
21.	刚好	gānghǎo	adj.	just right (as used in this story)
22.	赌气	dǔ qì	vo.	feel wronged and act rashly
23.	熬	áo	v.	endure; put up with
24.	道歉	dào qiàn	vo.	apologize; make an apology
25.	老子	lǎozi	n.	father(colloquial expression)
26.	要面子	yào miànzi	vo.	be concerned about face-saving; be sensitive about one's reputation
27.	开口	kāi kǒu	vo.	open one's mouth; start to talk
28.	死活	sǐhuó	adv.	anyway; no matter what
29.	有必要	yǒu bìyào	vo.	necessary

韩老师：**其实**谁都会有**犯错误**的时候，**包括大人**对孩子，我们不
　　　　能**总**拿"**知错就改**"这个**概念**来**教育**孩子，咱们当**家长**
　　　　的也要给孩子做个**榜样**嘛！

爸　爸：圆圆，对不起啊！是爸爸**错怪**你了，爸爸以后一定**改**。

妈　妈：圆圆，你看，爸爸都已经**承认**错误了，你就**原谅**他吧，啊！

妈　妈：哟，哎哟，这孩子。好了，**乖**，不哭了，你看，同学们都
　　　　笑话你了……

爸　爸：圆圆，圆圆！

30. 其实	qíshí	adv.	as a matter of fact; actually
31. 犯	fàn	v.	make(a mistake); commit(a crime)
32. 错误	cuòwù	n.	mistake; error
33. 包括	bāokuò	v.	include
34. 大人	dàren	n.	adult; grown-up
35. 总	zǒng	adv.	always
36. 知错就改	zhī cuò jiù gǎi		correct a mistake as soon as one realizes it
37. 概念	gàiniàn	n.	concept
38. 教育	jiàoyù	v.	teach; educate
39. 家长	jiāzhǎng	n.	parent or guardian of a child
40. 榜样	bǎngyàng	n.	example; model
41. 错怪	cuòguài	v.	wrong (someone)
42. 改	gǎi	v.	change; correct
43. 承认	chéngrèn	v.	admit (a mistake)
44. 原谅	yuánliàng	v.	forgive; pardon
45. 乖	guāi	adj.	(of a child)obedient; well-behaved; be good
46. 笑话	xiàohua	v./n.	laugh at; joke

妈　妈：哎，爸爸叫你呢。

爸　爸：圆圆，爸爸以后再怪你的话，就是小狗！"汪""汪""汪"！

47. 小狗	xiǎogǒu	n.	little dog
48. 汪	wāng	ono.	（onomatopoeia；sound that dogs make）

注释 Notes

1. **副词 "就"：**

    副词 "就" 有时表示 "只" 的意思。

    "就"，adverb，means "only" here.

    (1) 我呀，什么都不缺，就缺钱。

    I don't need anything but money.

    (2) 那个班的学生都去看电影了，就小李没去。

    Everyone in the class but Xiao Li went to the movie.

    (3) 今天我就有三节课。

    I only have three classes today.

2. **反问句（二）：**

    本课的反问句很多。

    There are quite a few rhetorical questions in this lesson. For example：

    (1) 不就是夏令营吗？这出门呀，又不是出国。

    （妈妈说话的意思是：只是去夏令营，不是去很远的地方、用很长时间，所以不需要花很多钱。You are only going to a summer camp, which is not far away, and which doesn't last long，so you don't need much money. ）

    (2) 我这不是跟你逗着玩儿呢嘛。

    （意思是：我这是跟你逗着玩儿，不是真的。I am only kidding you, not being serious. ）

    (3) 你还绝对呢……

    （意思是：你不要说 "绝对" 了，我不相信你。Don't say "absolutely" again，I don't trust you anymore. ）

    (4) 这事情还没搞清楚呢，你怎么能瞎怀疑孩子啊？

    （意思是：……你不应该随便怀疑孩子。..., you should not suspect the child without any evidence. ）

    (5) 这孩子一走就是好几天，这几天她怎么熬啊？

    （意思是：……这几天她没有办法熬/很难熬。How can she bear this

feeling (of being wronged) in the next few days?)

(6) 哪儿有老子给孩子道歉的？

（意思是：没有爸爸给孩子道歉的。A father should never apologize to his child.）

(7) 这点儿小事有必要吗？

（意思是：这点儿小事没有必要。It's not worth apologizing for such a trivial matter.）

3. **"又"**：

副词"又"的用法比较复杂，下面句子中"又"的作用是加强否定的语气。

"又", adverb, has a rather complicated usage. In the following sentences, it functions to emphasize the negative tone.

(1) 不就是夏令营吗？又不是出国。

You are only going to a summer camp, not going abroad, right?

(2) 我又没说你，你哭什么？

Why are you crying? I am not scolding you.

(3) 他又不是老师，你问他干什么？

He is not a teacher, why did you ask him?

4. **"劲儿"**：

"劲儿"用在形容词后边，可以描写神情、态度，类似"样子"。

"劲儿" often used after an adjective, describes some sort of expression, look or attitude, similar to "样子".

(1) 小气劲儿的，我这不是跟你逗着玩儿呢嘛。

Such a miser, I am only kidding you!

(2) 这次考试他考得非常好，你看他那高兴劲儿。

He did really well at the test. Just look how pleased he is with himself!

(3) 房间这么乱，懒劲儿！

Your room is a mess. What a lazybones!

5. **"你还绝对呢"**：

意思是：你还说绝对呢（你不应该说"绝对"）。

"你还绝对呢"：The speaker means to say "you shouldn't say 'absolutely'".

6. **起连接作用的"那"**：

"那" here functions as a discourse connector to link the meaning of the previous sentence with that of the current one.

（1）爸爸：……她哪儿来的钱？

Baba：Where is her money from？

妈妈：那她有钱也不一定是你那钱哪？

Mama：The money she has is not necessarily yours！

（2）你说我们不去南京，那我们去哪儿呀？

You said that we were not going to Nanjing，then where are we going？

（3）A：你这个办法不好。

Your idea didn't seem to work.

B：那你说怎么办？

Then you tell me what we should do.

7. 起承接作用的"就"：

"就"的用法也比较复杂。它在具有假设、让步、目的、因果等关系的复句或紧缩句里，起承接的作用，出现在第二个分句或紧缩句的第二部分。

"就" has several functions，one of which is to form a connecting link in the text in terms of logic relation. It is often seen in sentences containing hypothetical condition，cause-effect relation，concession，etc. It occurs before the verb of the second clause.

（1）这就怪了。（意思是：如果是这样，就奇怪了。）

In that case，it's really strange.

（2）因为你没来，所以会就没开。

Since you didn't come，we cancelled the meeting.

（3）你不喜欢看电影咱们就去跳舞。

Let's go dancing since you don't like movies.

8. "来着"：

用在动词后表示动作曾（在不久前）发生。口语。

"来着" is attached after an action verb，indicating that the action took place a moment ago.

（1）对呀，没错，我找我的日记本来着，可是没看见有什么钱呀。

You are right，I was just now looking for my diary，but I didn't see any money.

（2）刚才你说什么来着？我没听见。

What did you just say？I didn't hear.

有时忘了某事，也可以用"来着"。

Occasionally, "来着" is used to suggest a lapse of memory.

（3）那条街叫什么来着？我想不起来了。

What's the name of the street? I can't remember it now.

9. "什么":

参见第一课注释12。

"什么" can be used together with a noun to represent an indefinite person or an entity. In this case, "什么" functions to soften the tone, and will not change the meaning of the sentence.

（1）我找我的笔记本来着，可是没见有什么钱啊。

I looked for my notebook, but didn't see any money.

（2）他刚来不久，在这里没什么朋友。

He arrived here recently and hasn't made many friends.

（3）冰箱里没有什么吃的了。

There is almost no food in the refrigerator.

10. "还"（一）：

表示"没有想到"的语气，见第三课注释11。本课出现的"还"没有赞叹的意味。

"还" in this lesson expresses a feeling of surprise or disbelief. Please refer to note 11 of Lesson 3 for other usages.

你还真怀疑我拿你的钱啦？

You're really suspecting me of stealing your money?! (I cannot believe it)

11. "连吃的东西都没有带":

见第三课注释4"连……都/也……"。本剧中"你看看，这，她连吃的东西都没有带，我得给她送过去"的意思是：小孩子出门，带吃的东西是最基本的、最不容易忘记的，但是由于圆圆生气，所以连吃的东西都忘记带了。

Please refer to note 4 of Lesson 3 for the function of this grammatical pattern "连……都/也……". In this lesson, when Yuanyuan's mother says "你看看，这，她连吃的东西都没有带，……"（ "Look—she didn't even bring anything to eat"）she means to emphasize that Yuanyuan was so upset that she didn't even bring her food.

12. "倒":

副词"倒"有很多用法，本课的"倒"表示"和事实相反"的意思。

"倒", adverb, also has several functions. "倒" in this lesson is used to indicate that the situation mentioned (at the beginning of the sentence in the following examples) differs from reality.

(1) 你说得倒轻巧，这孩子一走就是好几天，这几天她怎么熬啊？

Easy for you to say. She will be gone for a few days. How can she stand this (being wronged)?

(2) 他想的倒好，哪有天上掉馅儿饼的事儿。

What a nice thought, but money doesn't grow on trees.

(3) 他说的倒好听，可就是不做。

She speaks nicely but never does anything.

13. **"死"：**

用在动词前表示"坚决"。口语。

"死", adverb, is used before a verb, i. e., 死 ＋ Verb, to indicate someone's, stubbornness. It is a colloquial expression.

(1) 他这个人呀，死要面子。

For him, there is nothing more important than his reputation.

(2) 他做错了事，死不承认。

He would never admit any mistakes.

14. **"死活"：**

表示"无论如何""不管怎样"的意思。口语。

"死活", also a colloquial expression, meaning "no matter what".

(1) 明天要考试，他死活要去看电影。

Tomorrow there is a test, but he wants to go see a movie no matter what.

(2) 她男朋友想跟她结婚，她死活不同意。

Her boyfriend wants to marry her, but she simply doesn't want to get married.

(3) 这个电话号码我告诉了他很多遍，可他死活记不住。

I told him this phone number many times, but he just couldn't remember it.

听说练习　**Listening & Speaking Exercises**

■ 一、课文理解 Text Comprehension

（一）根据故事情节选择适当的答案

Please choose the most appropriate answer based on the story

1. 圆圆要出门（　　）

　　A. 买东西　　　　　　B. 上学　　　　　　C. 去夏令营

2. 圆圆说她（　　　）

　　A. 缺吃的东西　　　　B. 缺钱　　　　　　C. 什么都不缺

3. 爸爸的钱放在＿＿＿＿＿了。（　　）

　　A. 抽屉里　　　　　　B. 桌子上　　　　　C. 他的衣服兜里

4. 圆圆开爸爸的抽屉是为了（　　　）

　　A. 找钱　　　　　　　B. 找她的日记本　　C. 什么都没有找

5. 圆圆说她的钱是＿＿＿＿＿给的。（　　　）

　　A. 妈妈　　　　　　　B. 姥姥　　　　　　C. 爸爸

6. 圆圆离开家的时候忘了带＿＿＿＿＿了。（　　　）

　　A. 钱　　　　　　　　B. 吃的东西　　　　C. 衣服

7. 爸爸开始不同意向圆圆道歉，因为他觉得（　　　）

　　A. 圆圆不应该翻他的抽屉

　　B. 大人不应该向孩子道歉

　　C. 他要请圆圆吃肯德基

8. 圆圆的老师认为（　　　）

　　A. 这是一件小事

　　B. 不管是大人还是孩子都应该"知错就改"

　　C. 孩子应该"知错就改"

（二）根据课文判断下面句子意思的正误

State whether the following statements are true or false based on the story

1. （　　）圆圆要去几天夏令营。
2. （　　）圆圆还缺一些钱。
3. （　　）圆圆昨天翻爸爸的抽屉要找钱。
4. （　　）圆圆的爸爸真的怀疑圆圆拿了他的钱。
5. （　　）圆圆的妈妈知道圆圆肯定没拿爸爸的钱。
6. （　　）圆圆的妈妈把钱放在圆圆爸爸的衣服兜里面了。
7. （　　）圆圆的妈妈让圆圆的爸爸去给圆圆送饭。
8. （　　）圆圆的爸爸很不好意思向圆圆道歉。

（三）先听故事叙述，然后复述故事

Listen to the narrative first and then retell the story

　　圆圆要去夏令营了。妈妈帮圆圆准备好行李正要出门的时候，爸爸发现他的钱找不到了。他怀疑圆圆拿了他的钱，因为他昨天看见圆圆翻他的抽屉了。圆圆告诉爸爸她翻抽屉是为了找日记本，没有看到爸爸的钱，但是爸爸不相信圆圆的话。圆圆觉得爸爸冤枉了她，赌气走了，连妈妈给她准备的吃的东西都没有带。这个时候，爸爸在他自己的衣（服）兜里找到了钱。爸爸觉得很不好意思——是他错怪了圆圆。他想去给圆圆道歉，但是又怕丢面子。最后，在妈妈和老师的帮助下，爸爸向圆圆道了歉，圆圆也原谅了爸爸。

■ 二、词语使用 Application of Vocabulary and Grammar

（一）选择题

Choose the item that is grammatically correct

1. 你怎么带这么多衣服呀？现在 ＿＿＿＿＿＿不是冬天，这些衣服绝对没有用。

    A. 只　　　　　　　B. 又　　　　　　　C. 还

2. A：你把我的车钥匙放在哪儿了？

    B：我＿＿＿＿＿＿放在厨房的桌子上了！

    A. 也　　　　　　　B. 又　　　　　　　C. 就

3. A：今天上午我给你打了好几个电话你怎么都没接？

    B：我上午上课＿＿＿＿＿＿。

    A. 来着　　　　　　B. 忙着　　　　　　C. 好久

4. A：明天的考试，你不用花很长时间准备，看看书就行了。

   B：你说得_____容易。

   　　A. 就　　　　　　　B. 倒　　　　　　　C. 也

5. A：要是你的朋友跟你借了钱不还，你怎么办？

   B：那我就提醒他还钱。_____借钱不还的？

   　　A. 怎么　　　　　　B. 为什么　　　　　C. 哪儿有

（二）选择题

Circle the answer that best reflects the meaning of the sentence

1. 不就是夏令营吗？又不是出国。（　　　）

   A. 只是去夏令营，不是出国去很远的地方，在外边住很长时间

   B. 去夏令营没有出国有意思

   C. 只打算去夏令营，没有打算出国

   D. 去夏令营比出国近得多

2. 就你这脑子啊，指不定放在哪儿了呢。（　　　）

   A. 你的脑子可能有问题，可能你忘了放在哪儿了

   B. 你的脑子不好，你别找了

   C. 你的记性不好，不一定放在哪儿（想不起来）了

   D. 你的脑子有问题，你总是找不到东西

3. 她哪儿来的钱哪？（　　　）

   A. 她在哪儿挣钱？

   B. 她的钱是从哪儿来的？她怎么会有钱？

   C. 她的钱放在哪儿了？

   D. 她从哪儿找到的钱？

4. 昨天晚上我找我的日记本来着。（　　　）

   A. 昨天晚上我找过我的日记本

   B. 昨天晚上我要找我的日记本

   C. 我是昨天晚上找日记本的

   D. 昨天晚上我正在找日记本

5. 你还真怀疑我偷你的钱啦？（　　　）

   A. 你又怀疑我偷你的钱了！

   B. （没有想到）你真怀疑我偷你的钱了！

   C. 你为什么怀疑我偷你的钱？

D. 你认为我会偷你的钱吗？

6. 你瞧瞧我这记性。（　　　）

    A. 你看我的记性真不好

    B. 你看看我的记性怎么样

    C. 你看我的记性好不好？

    D. 你知道我的记性不好

7. 他想跟圆圆认错，但死活说不出口。（　　　）

    A. 他想跟圆圆道歉，但是他不知道说什么

    B. 无论如何，他都不想跟圆圆道歉

    C. 他想跟圆圆道歉，但是他真不好意思开口跟圆圆说

    D. 让他跟圆圆道歉，除非他死了

8. 我们不能总拿"知错就改"这个概念来教育孩子，咱们当家长的也要给孩子做个榜样嘛！（　　　）

    A. 家长要求孩子"知错就改"，自己应该先这样做

    B. 家长应该只要求孩子"知错就改"

    C. 孩子得"知错就改"，家长应该学习孩子

    D. 家长总是孩子的榜样

（三）选择适当的词语，改写句中的画线部分

Choose the most appropriate words to replace the underlined parts

A. 指不定	B. 明明	C. 瞎怀疑	D. 绝对
E. 连……都……	F. 你瞧瞧我这记性	G. 错怪了我	H. 承认错误

1. 真奇怪，我清楚地记得把我的新 iPod 放在抽屉里了，怎么一下子就不见了？你看见了吗？

2. 你不应该随便就认为别人拿你的东西，我从来没有见过你的 iPod。我想，你可能把它忘在什么地方了。

3. 我肯定拿回来了，因为回家的时候，我一边走路一边听 iPod。

4. 啊！我的 iPod！我的记性真糟糕！我忘了，我回家以后在床上躺着听了一会儿音乐。谢谢！

5. 别谢我，以后你的东西你得记住放在哪儿了。上次你的中文书丢了，就差点儿以为是我拿了。

6. 对不起，我向你道歉。周末我请你吃肯德基！

（四）用所给词语完成对话

Complete the following dialogues with the items provided in the parenthesis

1.（死活，发誓）

A：你怎么跟男朋友分手了？

B：我们不是一种人。我爱打球，他爱看打球。每次我让他跟我一起去打球，他＿＿＿＿＿都不去。这么懒的人！我＿＿＿＿＿不想再见到他了！

2.（来着，绝对）

A：你想好点什么菜了吗？我们点菜吧！今天我请你。

B：＿＿＿＿＿不行！上次你已经请了我。今天该我请你了。哎，服务员呢？

A：刚才还在这儿＿＿＿＿＿。

3.（哪儿来的，你瞧瞧我这记性）

A：这本书真有用，我想知道的生词，书里边都有。

B：你这本书＿＿＿＿＿？

A：不是你让我买的吗？你忘了？

B：＿＿＿＿＿，我真的忘了！

4.（怎么了，错怪，瞎怀疑）

A：你＿＿＿＿＿？这么不高兴。

B：我男朋友一个周末都没有给我打电话。你说他会不会……

A：别＿＿＿＿＿了！上次你就＿＿＿＿＿他了。

（五）角色扮演 Role play

Make a dialogue with a classmate. One party plays Uncle Wang, and the other plays the young man. Your dialogue should incorporate the provided items.

爸爸	圆圆
You were so upset because you cannot find the ＄100 you just laid on the computer desk. You question your young daughter about the money because you saw her playing on the computer just now. A moment later, you found the money	Innocent as you were, you tried to tell your dad that you didn't even see the money. You swear to him that you absolutely had no idea about the money. When your dad apologized to you, you gladly forgave him.

in your pocket. You apologized to your daughter and promise to take her to KFC.	
1. 明明　　　　2. V 来着 3. 瞧瞧我这记性　4. 错怪	1. 连 V 都没 V　2. 发誓 3. 绝对　　　　4. 原谅

三、课堂讨论 Discussion

1. 如果你是圆圆的爸爸，你的钱找不到了，你会怎么问她？
2. 家长对孩子做错了事，应该怎样承认错误？
3. 你觉得孩子喜欢什么样的家长？
4. 圆圆的爸爸是不是一个好家长？为什么？

第五课 如此 "下载"

Can This Be Called "Download"

 编剧：苏溯

人物 (Characters)

杨露（Yáng Lù）——女，大学生。

陈卉（Chén Huì）——女，杨露的同学、**舍友**。

胡老师（Hú lǎoshī）——男，杨露和陈卉的老师。

课 文 Text

杨　露：陈卉。

陈　卉：嗯。

杨　露：胡老师**布置**的**论文**你打算怎么**弄**啊？

---

1. 如此	rúcǐ	pron.	such; this kind of
2. 下载	xiàzài	v.	download
3. 舍友	shèyǒu	n.	dormmate; roommate
4. 布置	bùzhì	v.	assign (homework, etc.)
5. 论文	lùnwén	n.	thesis; dissertation; paper
6. 弄	nòng	v.	do; handle; deal with (colloq.)

陈　卉：哎哟，**正**都**闷**着呢[N1]，**题目**太难了。哎，为**伊消**得人**憔悴**[N2]。

杨　露：**蓦然回首**，那人正在**灯火阑珊处**[N3]。你呀，**活人**还让**尿憋死**？[N4]**再说**[N5]，现在已经是网络时代了。

陈　卉：**网络时代**？

杨　露：这你都不懂？[N6]就是"**全选**""**复制**"再"**粘贴**"呀。

陈　卉：那不成了"**天下文章一大抄**[N7]"啦？

杨　露：哎，你借那么多书**干吗**？

7.	正	zhèng	adv.	right in the middle of (an action or a state)
8.	郁闷	yùmèn	adj.	gloomy, depressed; be gloomy, be depressed
9.	题目	tímù	n.	topic
10.	伊	yī	pron.	she; her (archaic)
11.	消	xiāo	v.	become thinner (literary)
12.	憔悴	qiáocuì	adj.	haggard, sallow; pined away
13.	蓦然	mòrán	adv.	suddenly; abruptly
14.	回首	huí shǒu	vo.	turn one's head; turn around (literary)
15.	灯火	dēnghuǒ	n.	lights
16.	阑珊	lánshān	v.	waning; coming to an end (literary)
17.	处	chù	n.	place; location
18.	活人	huórén	n.	living person
19.	尿	niào	n.	urine
20.	憋死	biē si	vc.	be suffocated to death
21.	网络	wǎngluò	n.	internet; network
22.	时代	shídài	n.	age; era; epoch
23.	全选	quán xuǎn		select all
24.	复制	fùzhì	v.	copy
25.	粘贴	zhāntiē	v.	paste
26.	文章	wénzhāng	n.	writing
27.	抄	chāo	v.	copy; plagiarize; plagiary
28.	干吗	gànmá	pron.	for what; what to do (colloq.)

陈　卉：写论文哪。

杨　露：**看来**[N8]呀，你还真想大干一场啦？[N9]

陈　卉：写论文又不是写**情书**，**随便划拉**一篇就行了。哎，我**想起**一件大事。

杨　露：什么事啊？

陈　卉：嗯，有人**托**我给你带一封信。是不是……嗯？我先看看了。

杨　露：哎，你给我。不许看。不能看我的信……

杨　露：他这情书写得太有**水平**了，我怎么看，怎么有一种**意犹未尽**的**感觉**[N10]……

陈　卉：哎，我说，你怎么不写论文**光**看情书啊？明天可就要**交**了啊，你也不着急？

杨　露：论文啊，我早写完了！

陈　卉：写完了？你什么时候写的呀？我怎么不知道啊？

29.	看来	kàn lái		it appears; it seems
30.	干	gàn	v.	do; work
31.	情书	qíngshū	n.	love letter
32.	随便	suíbiàn	adv.	random, casual; randomly, casually
33.	划拉	huála	v.	scribble
34.	想起	xiǎng qǐ	vc.	think of; recall
35.	托	tuō	v.	entrust (somebody to do something)
36.	水平	shuǐpíng	n.	level; proficiency; sophistication
37.	意犹未尽	yì yóu wèi jìn		not having one's meaning/emotion fully expressed
38.	感觉	gǎnjué	n.	feeling
39.	光	guāng	adv.	only; merely
40.	交	jiāo	v.	hand in

杨　露：陈卉，太好了！我刚才**碰见**胡老师了，我问他我那篇论文怎么样，你猜**怎么着**[N11]？我得**满分**了！

陈　卉：真的啊？可**据我所知**，胡老师他不会**轻易**给人满分的。

杨　露：哎，你怎么了？

陈　卉：我论文没过！你就**厉害**啦，写得又快，**成绩**又好，你有什么**秘诀**呀？

杨　露：就是"全选""复制"再"粘贴"就 OK 了！

陈　卉：啊？你的论文……真的是抄的？

杨　露：那不叫抄，那叫下载。现在都是网络时代了，**资源共享**嘛……

41.	碰见	pèng jiàn	vc.	meet unexpectedly; run into
42.	怎么着	zěnmezhe	pron.	what happened?
43.	满分	mǎn fēn		full score
44.	据我所知	jù wǒ suǒ zhī		to my knowledge
45.	轻易	qīngyì	adv.	easily; lightly
46.	厉害	lìhai	adj.	formidable; powerful
47.	成绩	chéngjì	n.	grade; mark; achievement
48.	秘诀	mìjué	n.	secret of success; knack
49.	资源	zīyuán	n.	resources
50.	共享	gòngxiǎng	v.	share; sharing

陈　卉：写点儿自己的东西，**表达**点儿自己的**看法**有什么不好的呀？……我觉得你这样做，**不仅**对不起胡老师，也对不起你自己。

杨　露：有那么严重吗？……**行了**行了，别**生气**了，我请你吃饭去，走。

杨　露：你是我**挂**在**天空**的一**道彩虹**……**绝了**[N12]**嘿**！哎，你说，我该怎么给他回呢？

陈　卉：你不会是想下载一篇情书吧？

杨　露：哎，对呀，哎，陈卉，你快来看啊！**排**在**纯情**篇**之**十大情书**之首**，我给你读啊，你是挂在我天边的一道彩虹……啊！下载的啊？**完全**一样，什么情书**高手**啊，骗子！

51.	表达	biǎodá	v.	express
52.	看法	kàn·fǎ	n.	opinion; point of view
53.	不仅	bùjǐn	adv.	not only
54.	行了	xíng le		enough of it; stop it
55.	生气	shēng qì	vo.	angry; get angry
56.	挂	guà	v.	hang
57.	天空	tiānkōng	n.	sky
58.	道	dào	m.	(a measure word for lines, stripes, rainbows, etc.)
59.	彩虹	cǎihóng	n.	rainbow
60.	绝了	jué le		beyond compare
61.	嘿	hei	interj.	(used to call attention)
62.	排	pái	v.	rank
63.	纯情	chúnqíng	n.	pure feeling; innocent love
64.	之	zhī	part.	(archaic and literary form for 的 indicating a possessive relationship)
65.	首	shǒu	n.	head; first place
66.	完全	wánquán	adv.	complete, whole; completely, wholly
67.	高手	gāoshǒu	n.	master hand

陈　卉：怎么样？被人欺骗的感觉不好受吧？

胡老师：杨露。

杨　露：胡老师。

胡老师：那天在办公室人太多，有些话没法跟你细说，你这次考试不及格！

杨　露：您那天不（是）告诉我得的是……

胡老师：听我说，那天给的满分，是为你下载的那个论文给的评价，你没想到吧，论文的作者是我当年读研的导师。

杨　露：啊……

胡老师：但是，有一条很遗憾，其中有一段很重要的文字你给弄丢

68.	欺骗	qīpiàn	v.	cheat; deceive
69.	好受	hǎoshòu	adj.	comfortable
70.	没法	méi fǎ		unable
71.	细说	xì shuō		say in detail
72.	不及格	bù jígé		fail (an exam); flunk
73.	评价	píngjià	v. /n.	appraise, assess; appraisal, assessment
74.	作者	zuòzhě	n.	writer; author
75.	当年	dāngnián	t.	that year (in the past)
76.	读研	dú yán	vo.	study as a graduate student
77.	导师	dǎoshī	n.	mentor; adviser
78.	遗憾	yíhàn	adj.	regret; regrettable
79.	其中	qízhōng	n.	amid it; among them
80.	段	duàn	m.	section; paragraph; passage
81.	文字	wénzì	n.	written words; writing
82.	弄丢	nòng diū	vc.	lose; mislay

了。杨露，我们虽然已经**进入**了网络时代，但是，不能什么都复制吧。咱们**无论**是做**学问**还是做人，总**要真诚**^{N13}，你说对吗？

杨　露：嗯……

83.	进入	jìnrù	v.	enter；get into
84.	无论	wúlùn	conj.	whether... or...
85.	学问	xuéwen	n.	learning；knowledge；scholarship
86.	要	yào	modal.	must
87.	真诚	zhēnchéng	adj.	sincere；earnest

注释 Notes

1. **"正……呢"和"正……着呢":**

　　"正……呢"表示动作正在进行。"着"表示状态的持续。"正……着呢"表示某种状态正在持续。

"正……呢"and " 正……着呢": The structure "正……呢"indicates an ongoing action, while the particle "着"denotes the continuation of a situation. The pattern "正……着呢"stresses the ongoingness of an action or condition.

（1）我正郁闷着呢。

　　I'm feeling depressed at this moment.

（2）别找他，他正烦着呢。

　　Don't bother him. He is feeling upset.

（3）很快就要放假了，她正高兴着呢，老师打电话来说她论文没通过。

　　Semester was to end soon and she was being happy, when the professor told her in a phone call that her thesis had failed.

2. **"为伊消得人憔悴":**

　　出自宋代柳永的词《蝶恋花》。原词如下：

凤栖梧

　　伫倚危楼风细细，望极春愁，黯黯生天际。草色烟光残照里。无言谁会凭阑意。　　拟把疏狂图一醉，对酒当歌，强乐还无味。衣带渐宽终不悔，为伊消得人憔悴。

This line is from the Song poet Liu Yong's (987～1053) *ci* in the tune of "Phoenix on the Wutong Tree"：

I stood on the towering building, in the gentle breeze,
And looked afar to the end of the horizon
Where spring longings faintly arose.

Amid the blur of green plants, dusk mist, and the twilight,

Who knew the heart of the one silently leaning on the railings?

For a moment I wanted to abandon myself and get drunk,

Raising the goblet amid the singing,

Yet dull it would be to force merrymaking.

My garments were getting loose, but I never regretted.

It was for her that I was becoming pined away.

——Trans. , Liangyan Ge

"衣带渐宽终不悔，为伊消得人憔悴"的意思：为了他，虽然觉得衣服越来越肥大，人一天比一天瘦，但是从来不后悔。本剧人物用的后面一句，意思是说她正为了写论文而发愁。

In the play, Chen Hui cites the final line of the poem to express her worry and anxiety about the writing of her thesis.

3. **"蓦然回首，那人正在灯火阑珊处"**：

出自宋代诗人辛弃疾的词《青玉案》。

青玉案·元夕

东风夜放花千树，更吹落、星如雨。宝马雕车香满路，凤箫声动，玉壶光转，一夜鱼龙舞。　　蛾儿雪柳黄金缕，笑语盈盈暗香去。众里寻他千百度，蓦然回首，那人却在，灯火阑珊处。

This line is from the Southern-Song poet Xin Qiji's (1140~1207) *ci* "Lantern Festival" in the tune "Green Jade Cup":

One night's east wind made a thousand trees burst into flowers,

And breathe down still more

Showers of fallen stars.

Splendid horses, carved carriages, fragrance filled the road.

Music resounded from paired flutes,

Light swirled on water-clock towers.

All night long, the fabled fish-dragons danced.

Gold-threaded jacket, moth- or willow-shaped hair ornaments

Melted into the throng, giggling, a trail of scents.

In the crowed I looked for her a thousand and one times,

And all at once, as I turned my head,

I was startled to find her

Among the lanterns where candles were growing dim.

—Trans., Irving Y. Lo. *Sunflower Splendor* (Bloomington：Indiana University Press，1975), pp. 394～395.

"众里寻他千百度，蓦然回首，那人却在灯火阑珊处"的意思是：在人群中千百次地找他，一回头却在灯光昏暗的地方看见了他。本剧用了后面一句，意思是：你很容易就能找到要找的东西。

The final line of the poem is cited in the play, where it means：You have been seeking something assiduously but you may find it in a very unlikely place unexpectedly.

4. **"活人还让尿憋死"**：

俗语。这是个反问句，意思是：活人不能让尿憋死。比喻不应该让一点小事难倒，应该想办法解决。

This is a rhetorical question，which literally means that a living person should not be killed by his bursting bladder. As a colloquial expression，it refers metaphorically to a situation in which one should not be overwhelmed by a minor problem and should be able to find a solution for it.

5. **"再说"**：

连词。用于进一步说明原因。

"再说"：It is a conjunction that introduces a further explanation of the reason.

(1) 你呀，活人还让尿憋死？再说，现在已经是网络时代了。

Look at you! Can a living person die from his pent-up urine? Besides，it is now the internet age.

(2) A：我们去看电影好吗？

Shall we go to see a movie?

B：我不想去，现在没有什么好电影，再说外边正在下雨。

I don't want to. There are no good movies. Besides，it's raining now.

(3) 你不要给她打电话了。她很忙，再说她说过她不喜欢你。

Don't call her, she is busy. Besides，she said she didn't like you.

6. **"这你都不懂"**:

这句话和"连这个你都不懂"意思一样，见第三课注释4。

Here "这" is equivalent to "连这个". See note 4 in Lesson 3.

7. **"天下文章一大抄"**:

俗语，意思是：大家写文章都是互相抄来抄去。

As a popular saying, it suggests—unfairly perhaps—that most writers compose their writings by plagiarizing each other.

8. **"看来"**:

是一个插入语，表示说话人根据某种情况（一般是当前的情况或正在谈论的事情的情况）估计、推测。

"看来" is a parenthesis that introduces the speaker's assumption or judgment (based on the current circumstances or the situation under discussion).

(1) 打雷了，看来要下雨。

It's thundering. It looks like raining.

(2) A：我的女朋友去中国了，她要我下个月一定去。

My girlfriend went to China. She wants me to go there next month.

B：看来你只有这个月能在我们这里工作了。

So this seems to be your last month to work with us here.

(3) 杨露：哎，你借那么多书干吗？

Yang Lu：Hey, why did you borrow so many books?

陈卉：写论文哪。

Chen Hui：Because I'm writing a thesis.

杨露：看来呀，你还真想大干一场啦？

Yang Lu：It seems you really want to have a big go at it.

9. **"你还真想大干一场啦"**:

"还"表示出乎意料的语气，见第一课注释4。

Do you really want to have a big go at it? Here "还" denotes a tone of surprise. Also see note 4 in Lesson 1.

10. **"我怎么看，怎么有一种意犹未尽的感觉"**:

这里连用两个"怎么"表示"无论/不管……"或"越……越……"的意思。上面这个句子的意思是：（这封情书）我无论怎么看，都有一种意犹未尽的感觉。或者：我越看，越有一种意犹未尽的感觉。

The function of the pattern "怎么……怎么……"in the sentence above

is quite similar to that of the structure "无论/不管……" or "越……越
……". The sentence can thus be paraphrased as: No matter how I read
(the love letter), I have the feeling that the emotions are not fully expressed. Another way to paraphrase it could be: The more I read it, the
more I feel that the emotions are not fully expressed.

11. "怎么着":

"怎么着"有时是"怎么"的意思。

"怎么着" is sometimes interchangeable with "怎么"(why, how
come).

(1) 怎么着? 你不同意? (意思是: 怎么? 你不同意?)

Why? You don't agree?

在下面的句子中,"怎么着"是"怎么样"的意思。

In the sentence below, however, "怎么着" is closer to "怎么样"
(how).

(2) 我刚才碰见胡老师了,我问他我那篇论文怎么样,你猜怎么着,我得
满分了!

I bumped into Professor Hu a moment ago, and I asked him about my
thesis. You know what, I got a full score for it!

(3) 怎么着? 准备好了? (意思是: 怎么样? 准备好了?)

How is it? Are you ready now?

12. "绝了":

"绝"有"没有(人/东西)比得上"的意思,常用来称赞某种技艺、
手艺、表演等。一般出现于感叹句。口语。

As a colloquialism,"绝" has the meaning of being unrivaled and unsur-
passable. It is often used in a compliment on someone's skills or performance.

(1) 你是我挂在天空的一道彩虹……绝了嘿!

"You are a rainbow in the sky for me...." That's simply marvelous!

这个句子中的"绝了"是称赞前面的"诗句"写得好。

In Example (1),"绝了" is used in a praise of the poetic line "你是我挂
在天空的一道彩虹".

(2) 那个演员演得真是绝了。

That actor's performance was superb.

(3) 那个房子的设计真是绝了。

The layout of that house was incomparably ingenious.

13. **"无论……都……"：**

注意"无论"后边总是要用疑问形式，而且后边要有"都"与之呼应。

In the structure "无论……都……", what follows "无论" always appears in the interrogative form, which is always echoed by the adverb "都" in the latter clause.

(1) 咱们无论是做学问还是做人，总要真诚，你说对吗？

No matter as a scholar or as a person, one should always be sincere. Do you agree?

(2) 明天的会议无论谁去都可以。

To go to tomorrow's meeting, anyone would be fine.

(3) 你周末无论去不去看电影都打电话告诉我一下。

Whether you will see the movie or not this weekend, give me a phone call.

例（1）"咱们无论是做学问还是做人，总要真诚，你说对吗？"后一分句没有用"都"，而是用了一个意思近似的"总"。

In Example (1), "都" does not appear in the latter clause, but the word "总" (always) is used instead, which has a meaning quite similar to that of "都".

听说练习　Listening & Speaking Exercises

■ 一、课文理解 Text Comprehension

(一) 根据故事情节选择适当的答案

Please choose the most appropriate answer based on the story

1. 陈卉觉得郁闷是因为（　　　）
   A. 杨露学习比她好　　　B. 论文还没写好　　　C. 他没有电脑

2. 陈卉借了很多书是为了（　　　）
   A. 写情书　　　　　　　B. 写论文　　　　　　C. 大干一场

3. 明天就要交论文了，杨露为什么一点儿也不着急？（　　　）
   A. 论文已经交了　　　　B. 情书比论文重要　　C. 论文早写完了

4. 胡老师给谁的论文打了满分？（　　　）
   A. 杨露　　　　　　　　B. 陈卉　　　　　　　C. 他的导师

5. 杨露交的论文是（　　　）
   A. 她导师写的　　　　　B. 胡老师的导师写的　C. 她自己写的

6. 杨露认为现在是网络时代了，资源应该（　　　）
   A. 复制　　　　　　　　B. 共享　　　　　　　C. 下载

7. 杨露收到的情书是一个男人（　　　）
   A. 为她写的　　　　　　B. 为她抄的　　　　　C. 从网上下载的

8. 胡老师认为做什么要真诚？（　　　）
   A. 做人　　　　　　　　B. 做学问　　　　　　C. 做人和做学问

(二) 根据课文判断下面句子意思的正误

State whether the following statements are true or false based on the story

1.（　　　）题目太难了，杨露正在为写论文着急。

2.（　　　）陈卉为写论文借了很多书。

3.（　　　）给杨露情书的人写情书的水平很高。

4.（　　）杨露的论文得了满分。

5.（　　）陈卉认为杨露很厉害，论文写得又快，成绩又好。

6.（　　）杨露认为给她情书的人是骗子。

7.（　　）杨露认为在网络时代资源应该共享。

8.（　　）杨露交的的论文是胡老师的老师写的。

（三）先听故事叙述，然后复述故事

Listen to the narrative first and then retell the story

　　杨露和陈卉都是研究生。要交论文了，陈卉很着急，所以借了很多书，打算坐下好好来写。陈卉没看见杨露写论义，杨露却说她早就写完了。杨露还告诉陈卉她的秘诀就是"全选""复制"再"粘贴"。杨露说"现在已经是网络时代了，资源应该共享"，陈卉不同意她的看法。

　　杨露的男朋友叫陈卉带给杨露一封信，原来是封情书。杨露很快发现这位情书高手原来是个骗子！这封情书是从网上下载的。被人欺骗的感觉是很不好受的。

　　杨露以为自己的论文得了满分。没想到胡老师说那个满分是对她下载的那篇论文的评价，而论文的作者是胡老师当年读研的导师。胡老师告诉她无论是做学问还是做人，都要真诚。

■ 二、词语使用 Application of Vocabulary and Grammar

（一）选择题

Choose the item that is grammatically correct

1."全选""复制"再"粘贴"，那不　　　　　　　了"天下文章一大抄"啦？

　　A. 像　　　　　　　　　B. 是　　　　　　　　　C. 成

2. 你借了这么多书，　　　　　　　你还真想大干一场啦？

　　A. 看来　　　　　　　　B. 因为　　　　　　　　C. 所以

3. 写论文　　　　　　　不是写情书，随便划拉一篇就行了。

　　A. 又　　　　　　　　　B. 就　　　　　　　　　C. 但

4. 哎，我想　　　　　　　一件大事，有人托我给你带一封信，差点儿忘了。

　　A. 出　　　　　　　　　B. 起　　　　　　　　　C. 着

5. 写完了？你什么时候写的呀？我　　　　　　　不知道啊？

　　A. 这么　　　　　　　　B. 当然　　　　　　　　C. 怎么

6. 那天在办公室人太多，有些话没法跟你_____说，你这次考试不及格！

    A. 细   B. 慢   C. 都

7. 咱们_____是做学问还是做人，总要真诚。

    A. 或者   B. 还是   C. 无论

（二）选择题

Circle the answer that best reflects the meaning of the underlined portion of the sentence

1. 天下文章一大抄（　　　）

    A. 天下的文章都是一个人抄的

    B. 抄文章很重要

    C. 大家写文章都是互相抄来抄去

    D. 文章要多抄

2. 你借那么多书。看来呀，你还真想大干一场啦？（　　　）

    A. 坐下来好好写论文

    B. 跟同学好好比一比

    C. 跟老师好好干一下

    D. 只学习不睡觉

3. "蓦然回首，那人正在灯火阑珊处"（　　　）

    A. 当然

    B. 突然

    C. 自然

    D. 立刻

4. 那个演员演得真是绝了。（　　　）

    A. 到底了

    B. 没人比得上

    C. 没人学了

    D. 没人看了

5. 这篇情书排在纯情篇之十大情书之首。（　　　）

    A. 头上

    B. 第一

    C. 中间

D. 其中之一

6. 有人<u>托</u>我给你带一封信。（　　）

A. 帮

B. 把

C. 请

D. 替

（三）选择适当的词语，替换句中的画线部分

Choose the most appropriate words to replace the underlined parts

A. 碰见	B. 划拉	C. 郁闷
D. 绝了	E. 布置	F. 据我所知

1. 杨露：胡老师<u>要我们做</u>的题目太难了。马上要交了，你想怎么弄啊？

2. 陈卉：哎哟，正为这事<u>发愁</u>呢。

3. 他这情书写得<u>太有水平了</u>。

4. 写论文又不是写情书，随便<u>乱写</u>一篇就行了。

5. 我刚才<u>遇到</u>了胡老师，我那篇论文得了个满分！

6. 真的啊？<u>别人告诉我</u>胡老师他不会轻易给人满分的。

（四）用所给词语完成对话

Complete the following dialogues with the items provided in the parenthesis

1. （无论……都……，遗憾）

甲：你是个很有水平的学生，非常_____你做出这样的事情。

乙：以后_____我怎么忙，_____不会上网下载文章了。

2. （怎么着，据我所知）

甲：我刚才碰见赵叔叔了，我问他最近怎么样，你猜_____？他要结婚了！

乙：真的啊？可_____，他从来没有女朋友啊。

甲：你又不是一天二十四个小时跟他在一起，你怎么知道？

3. （绝了，看来）

甲：这封情书写得_____！_____他太爱你了，写这封信一定花了很多时间。

4. （再说，正 V 着呢）

甲：论文写完了吗？

乙：哎哟，我_____。几天没睡好觉了。

甲：活人还能让尿憋死？上网下载一篇交上去不得了。_____，不交论文也毕得了业。

（五）角色扮演 Role play

Make a dialogue with a classmate. One party plays Yang Lu，and the other plays Chen Hui. Your dialogue should incorporate the provided items.

杨露	陈卉
You see Chen Hui carrying a lot of books in preparation for writing her thesis. You tell her that it is now the Internet Age，one can easily download an article rather than having to labor over it. You happily tell Chen Hui that Teacher Hu has just told you that your thesis had been given full marks.	You have been under pressure to finish writing your thesis. Yang Lu claims that she has finished hers though you even didn't see her working on it. Her talk of "the Internet Age" does not impress you. When you hear from Yang Lu that Teacher Hu has given her thesis full marks，you are also told the "select all"，"copy" and "cut" scheme. You tell Yang Lu your thoughts on this practice.
1. 打算　　2. 活人还让尿憋死 3. 再说　　4. 网络时代 5. 大干一场 6. "全选""复制"再"粘贴" 7. 你猜怎么着 8. 资源共享	1. 正……着呢 2. 天下文章一大抄 3. 随便划拉一篇　　4. 托我 5. 据我所知　　6. 轻易 7. 有什么秘诀 8. 又……又…… 9. 不仅……也……

■ 三、课堂讨论 Discussion

1. 你对杨露说的"现在是网络时代，资源可以共享"有什么看法？

2. 你认为给杨露写情书的人是骗子吗？为什么？

3. 杨露是骗子吗？为什么？

4. 做学问、做人，真诚重要吗？

第六课 还得学

Long Way to Go

编剧：谢宝宝

人物 （Characters）

麦克（Màikè）——外国人，男，三十岁左右。

朱蒂（Zhūdì）——外国人，麦克的**妻子**。

老李（Lǎo Lǐ）——男，四十岁左右。

杨丽华（Yáng Lìhuá）——老李的妻子。

课　文　Text

老　李：**老婆**，我考考你今天咱们学的 English：嗯……You are my wife 是什么意思？

杨丽华：……

老　李：不知道了吧，我告诉你吧……

杨丽华：**反正**[N1]我就知道：You are my husband.

老　李：行啊，老婆！

杨丽华：那当然了。

1. 妻子	qīzi	n.	wife
2. 老婆	lǎopó	n.	wife
3. 反正	fǎnzhèng	adv.	anyway; in any case

老　李：哎，那不是那个咱们的**邻居**，那男的叫什么来着？

杨丽华：叫麦克，他**夫人**叫朱蒂，哎，**以后低头不见抬头见的**[N2]，咱过去打声**招呼**吧？

老　李：对，走！

杨丽华：Hi！Hello！……

麦　克：Hello！你们好！

老　李：你们吃了吗？

麦　克：吃？你问我吃了吗？

老　李：Yes，yes！

麦　克：Oh，Chinese people are so wonderful！They will invite us for dinner！（哇，中国人好热情啊！他们**邀请**咱们**共进晚餐**！）

杨丽华：你**听懂**了吗？

老　李：那……那"**再说一遍**"怎么说来着？哦，pardon，pardon？

朱　蒂：你们中国人**友好**、热情，谢谢你们请我们吃晚饭！**待会**儿见！

麦　克：Thank you. See you later.（谢谢，一会儿见！）

---

4. 邻居	línjū	n.	neighbor; people of the neighborhood
5. 夫人	fūren	n.	Mrs; wife
6. 以后	yǐhòu	t.	from now on; later on
7. 招呼	zhāohu	v./n.	greet; greeting
8. 邀请	yāoqǐng	v.	invite
9. 共进晚餐	gòng jìn wǎncān		eat dinner together
10. 听懂	tīng dǒng	vc.	understand
11. 遍	biàn	m.	(MW for action)
12. 友好	yǒuhǎo	adj.	friendly
13. 待会儿见	dāi huìr jiàn		see you later

老　李：**奇了怪了**[N3]，我没说请他们吃饭啊？

杨丽华：**还**[N4]说呢，不是就你说了**句**"吃了吗"！人家老外就以为咱们要请人吃饭呢。

老　李：这样也好，我呀，今天就给他们**露两手**[N5]，让他们也尝尝老北京的**家常菜**！

朱　蒂：哇！这么多吃的！真是太**香**了！Perfect！真地道！

老　李：朱蒂**女士**，麦克先生，别客气，please，please！

麦　克：I was so happy to accept the invitation! 我真高兴**接受**这个……

朱　蒂：……邀请！真是太棒了！

老　李：哪里哪里，这也就是我们的**家常便饭**，是吧。来来，别客气，吃吃。

14. 奇了怪了	qí le guài le		(see note 3)
15. 句	jù	m.	(a measure word for speech)
16. 露两手	lòu liǎng shǒu		(see note 5)
17. 家常菜	jiācháng cài	n.	homely dish
18. 香	xiāng	adj.	delicious
19. 女士	nǚshì	n.	lady；madam
20. 接受	jiēshòu	v.	accept
21. 家常便饭	jiācháng biànfàn		homely food

老　李：哎，对了，咱们**守着**^{N6}那么好的学习英语**条件**，咱怎么不**利用**利用呢？

杨丽华：什么条件啊？

老　李：**对门**麦克**两口子**，那是**现成**的**外教**啊？

杨丽华：对呀。

老　李：不行，哪天呢，我还得请这两口子好好地**撮一顿**。来人了，我去看看谁。

老　李：你好。

麦　克：你们好！今天晚上……吃了吗？

老　李：今天晚上？今天晚上还没到，我上哪里去吃啊？

朱　蒂：他是说，今天晚上想请你们吃饭。

老　李：好。

老　李：真香啊！Good！Very good！

朱　蒂：我刚学会了中国菜，尝尝我的**手艺**吧！你们都饿了吧？

老　李：不饿，不饿。

麦　克：不饿？那**难道**你们——吃了？

22.	守着	shǒu zhe		(see note 6)
23.	条件	tiáojiàn	n.	situation; environment
24.	利用	lìyòng	v.	make use of; take advantage of
25.	对门	duìmén	n.	across the hallway; (of two apartments) facing each other
26.	两口子	liǎngkǒuzi	n.	husband and wife; married couple
27.	现成	xiànchéng	adj.	readily available
28.	外教	wàijiào	n.	foreign teacher
29.	撮一顿	cuō yi dùn	vo.	have a good meal
30.	手艺	shǒuyì	n.	skill; craftsmanship
31.	难道	nándào	adv.	Is it possible that...; Do you really mean to say that...

老　李：没吃，没吃呢。

朱　蒂：没吃就好，快吃吧。

老　李：You are my teacher.

麦　克：No，we are friends.

老　李：No，No，不是这个意思。This is rice，ok?

麦　克：Yes!

杨丽华：Egg，tomato?

麦　克：Correct，yes!

老　李：所以，You are our teacher，English teacher.

麦　克：不，不，你们是我的老师，我想学你们中国的……steam cooking?

朱　蒂：中国的**烹调**。

老　李：没问题啊!

朱　蒂：我去帮你盛饭!

老　李：不，不，我**饱**了。Enough!

朱　蒂：Ok!

老　李：我说老婆，你没觉得我今天的这英语水平是**噌噌见长**[N7]?

杨丽华：**良师出高徒**嘛!

老　李：这要到了2008年**奥运会**，我这满肚子的**单词**和**句子**，到时**一打饱嗝**儿那出来就是英语啊。

32. 烹调	pēngtiáo	v.	cook
33. 饱	bǎo	adj.	eat till full; full
34. 噌噌见长	cēngcēng jiànzhǎng		(see note 7)
35. 良师出高徒	liáng shī chū gāo tú		a great teachers produces brilliant students; the teacher of enlightenment brings up disciples of accomplishment
36. 奥运会	Àoyùnhuì	N.	abbreviation of Olympic Games
37. 单词	dāncí	n.	vocabulary
38. 句子	jùzi	n.	sentence
39. 打饱嗝	dǎ bǎogé	vo.	belch

杨丽华：你呀，打不了饱嗝儿了，瞧你饿得这样，哪儿像刚吃完饭回来的呀？

老　李：你说这老外有多逗啊，我那是客气！哎，这朱蒂还真实在！我说不吃了，她还真就不让[N8]了。

杨丽华：他们没有中国人这么含蓄，人家的表达方式就是直接，饿就是饿，好吃就猛吃[N9]。看来呀，咱们还不能光学会外语，咱们还要掌握人家外国的风土人情和待人接物。

老　李：那倒是，要不到时候我还得挨饿。

40. 实在	shízài	adj. /adv.	true; honest
41. 含蓄	hánxù	adj.	subtle; reserved
42. 方式	fāngshì	n.	way; style
43. 直接	zhíjiē	adj.	direct
44. 饿	è	adj.	hungry
45. 学会	xué huì	vc.	learn; master
46. 外语	wàiyǔ	n.	foreign language
47. 掌握	zhǎngwò	v.	grasp; master
48. 风土人情	fēng tǔ rén qíng		local costumes
49. 待人接物	dài rén jiē wù		codes of conduct; codes of behavior
50. 要不	yàobù	conj.	otherwise; or else
51. 挨饿	ái è		be starved

注释　Notes

1. **"反正"**：

    副词。表示在任何情况下结论或结果都不改变，都一样。

    "反正", an adverb, means "anyway". It indicates that the result remains the same regardless of the situation.

    (1) 老李：不知道了吧，我告诉你……

    Lao Li：You really don't know, do you? Let me tell you…….

    杨丽华：反正我就知道：You are my husband.

    Yang Lihua：What I do know, in any case, is that *you are my husband*.

    杨丽华这句话的意思是：你说我什么没关系，但是我知道……

    This sentence means "I don't care what you said, but I understand what you meant."

    (2) 今天复习不复习没关系，反正明天不考试。

    It doesn't matter whether we review today or not. The test is not tomorrow anyway.

    (3) 明天的会你去不去都行，反正我得去。

    It's okay whether you go or not, but I simply have to go to the meeting tomorrow.

2. **"（以后）低头不见抬头见的，……"**：

    意思是说邻居、同事等在生活和工作中经常会遇到、见面。口语。

    "低头不见抬头见" means "neighbors or co-workers always see each other in everyday life or work". This expression implies that one needs to maintain a good relationship with his/her neighbors or co-workers.

3. **"奇了怪了"**：

    意思同"奇怪"，用了两个"了"有加重语气的作用。还可以说"多了去了""倒了霉了""发了大财了"等等。

    The meaning of "奇了怪了" is the same as "奇怪", except the former form, with two "了", puts more emphasis on the tone. The same is true with "多了去了" vs. "多了"，"倒了霉了" vs. "倒霉了"，"发了财了" vs. "发财了".

4. **副词"还"（二）：**

"还"可以表示"应该怎样而没有怎样"，包含责备或讽刺的语气。

"还" indicates that something is not what it's supposed to be.

It often implies a tone of blame or sarcasm.

(1) 老李：奇了怪了，我没说请他们吃饭啊？

Lao Li：That's the strangest thing! Did I say I would invite them to dinner?

杨丽华：还说呢，不是就你说了句"吃了吗"！人家老外就以为咱们要请人吃饭呢。

Yang Lihua：Speaking of which, isn't this all because you asked them "Have you eaten yet"? And the foreigners must've thought we're inviting them to dinner!

杨丽华说"还说呢"是在责备、埋怨老李不该说"吃了吗"。

By using "还说呢", Yang Lihua is blaming Lao Li.

(2) 还笑呢，看我的作业本都让你弄脏了。

And you're laughing! Look how dirty you got my workbook!

(3) A：我的钱包呢？

Where is my purse?

B：还问我，钱包不是在你的手上吗？

You ask me? Weren't you holding it?

5. **"露两手"：**

通常说"露一手"，意思是表现、显示一下某方面高超的本领。

"露两手", often said as "露一手", means to show off one's skill or talent.

(1) 我呀，今天就给他们露两手，让他们也尝尝老北京的家常菜！

Today I'm going to give them a good taste of home-made Beijing dishes!

(2) 小李，你篮球打得那么好，上去给他们露一手。

Xiao Li, you are such a good basketball player. Why don't you give them a show?

(3) 你歌唱得不错，今天在大家面前真是露了一手。

You sing really well. Today you were the center of everyone's attention.

6. **"守着"：**

有"靠近"的意思。口语。本剧中"咱们守着那么好的学习英语条件，咱怎么不利用利用呢"的意思是：咱们跟说英语的外国人是邻居，咱们正在学英语，应该跟邻居学英语。

The literal meaning of "守着" is "having someone/something right next to you". In this lesson，"咱们守着那么好的学习英语条件，咱怎么不利用利用呢?" means "We're sitting right next to a great opportunity to learn English，so why not take advantage of it?"

7. **"噌噌见长"：**

"见长"的意思是（高矮、大小等等）能看出来比以前"长了"。"噌噌"模拟声音，形容长得快，好像能听见长的时候的声音一样。

"见长" means "to appear taller or bigger". "噌噌" is an onomatopoeia，exaggerating the sound of growing.

8. **"让"：**

"让"有"请人接受招待"的意思。中国的传统是在请客人吃饭时，主人把请客人再吃、多吃，再喝、多喝作为一种礼貌。现在年轻人渐渐不再"让"了。否定形式"不用让了""别让了"用得较多。

"让" means "to invite（someone to eat）"，usually used when treating someone to a meal. It is a Chinese custom to invite the guest to eat（or drink）more during the meal to show hospitality. Nowadays the younger generation does not do this as much. The negative form of "让" i. e.，"不用让了"，or "别让了" is more frequently used.

（1）哎，这朱蒂还真实在！我说不吃了，她还真就不让了。

Hey，this Judie，she really takes people seriously. I said I wouldn't eat anything else，and then she didn't offer anymore.

（2）我们都吃饱了，你就不用让了。

We've all had enough. Please don't offer the food any more.

（3）别让了，我们不客气。

We'll make ourselves at home. Please don't be so polite.

9. **"饿就是饿，好吃就猛吃"：**

"人家的表达方式就是直接，饿就是饿，好吃就猛吃。"这句话的意思是：外国人表达方式很直接。如果饿了，就说饿了，如果东西好吃，就快吃、多吃。汉语的口语中很少用"如果……就……"、"因为……，所以……"等关联词语。所以很多句子的意思和句子之间的关系要靠上下文、语言环境来理解。

"人家的表达方式就是直接，饿就是饿，好吃就猛吃。"The speaker is

saying that the foreigners can be very straight-forward, that is, if they are hungry they would say so; and if they like the food they would eat a lot. Please notice that in colloquial speech such as this, the conjunctions "如果……就……", "因为……，所以……" are more often than not omitted. The addressee can, however, get the correct interpretation based on the context and extra-linguistic factors.

听说练习 Listening & Speaking Exercises

一、课文理解 Text Comprehension

（一）根据故事情节选择适当的答案

Please choose the most appropriate answer based on the story

1. 老李和杨丽华是麦克和朱蒂的（　　）

　　A. 朋友　　　　　　　　B. 同事　　　　　　　C. 邻居

2. 老李和杨丽华跟麦克和朱蒂打招呼是为了（　　）

　　A. 练习说英文　　　　B. 请他们吃饭　　　　C. 认识他们

3. 麦克和朱蒂以为老李和杨丽华想（　　）

　　A. 练习说英文

　　B. 请他们吃饭

　　C. 认识他们

4. 中国人说"吃了吗"是想（　　）

　　A. 请别人吃饭

　　B. 打招呼

　　C. 认识新朋友

5. 麦克对中国的_____有兴趣。（　　）

　　A. 烹调　　　　　　　　B. 书法　　　　　　　C. 文化

6. 老李在麦克家没有吃饱是因为他（　　）

　　A. 不喜欢麦克做的饭

　　B. 不好意思多吃

　　C. 担心打饱嗝儿

7. 中国人请客吃饭的时候一定要让客人（　　）

　　A. 别带礼物

　　B. 多吃、多喝

　　C. 喝酒

8. 如果老李和杨丽华再去麦克家吃饭，他们（　　　）

    A. 会含蓄一点儿

    B. 会说真话（没吃饱不能说吃饱了）

    C. 会挨饿

（二）根据课文判断下面句子意思的正误

State whether the following statements are true or false based on the story

1. （　　）老李和杨丽华打算请他们的新邻居吃饭。

2. （　　）麦克喜欢做中国饭。

3. （　　）老李和杨丽华到麦克家吃饭以前已经吃饭了。

4. （　　）老李在麦克家没吃饱。

5. （　　）朱蒂不想让老李吃得太多。

6. （　　）老李和杨丽华认识到，学英语的时候也要学外国文化。

（三）先听故事叙述，然后复述故事

Listen to the narrative first and then retell the story

    老李家的对门搬来了一家外国邻居，他们叫麦克和朱蒂。老李去跟新邻居打招呼。可是因为中国文化和外国的文化不一样，外国邻居以为老李来请他们吃饭。当麦克和朱蒂来的时候，老李和太太杨丽华很高兴地请他们吃了一顿中国饭。后来，麦克和朱蒂也请老李和他太太到他们家吃饭。可是，老李却没有吃饱，因为他不懂外国人的风土人情。后来，老李知道了，去外国朋友家吃饭，饿了就说饿了，好吃就多吃。

■ 二、词语使用 Application of Vocabulary and Grammar

（一）选择题

Choose the item that is grammatically correct

1. 以后我们跟他们就是邻居了，咱们过去打_____招呼吧！

    A. 遍   B. 声   C. 次   D. 回

2. 今天不管怎么样，我都得把功课做完，_____明天上午我没有课，可以起得晚一点儿。

    A. 反正   B. 反而   C. 虽然   D. 难道

3. 听说你的男朋友写汉字写得很漂亮，你让他给我们_____，怎么样？

    A. 看看   B. 露两手   C. 做个榜样   D. 打个招呼

4. 上个学期，我在北京学了一个学期的汉语。开始的几个星期，我觉得我的口语水平真 _____ 。

    A. 直接　　　　B. 含蓄　　　　C. 见长　　　　D. 地道

5. 你刚吃完午饭就饿了？ _____ 你吃饭的时候没吃饱吗？

    A. 反正　　　　B. 难道　　　　C. 当然　　　　D. 反而

6. 我的中国朋友告诉我，一般中国人表达爱情的方式比较 _____ ，男女朋友互相很少说"我爱你"。

    A. 直接　　　　B. 地道　　　　C. 客气　　　　D. 含蓄

（二）选择题

Circle the answer that best reflects the meaning of the sentence

1. 以后我们是邻居了，低头不见抬头见……（　　　）

    A. 以后我们是邻居了，会常常见面

    B. 以后我们是邻居了，见面的时候要低头

    C. 以后我们是邻居了，应该每天都见面

    D. 以后我们是邻居了，见面的时候要抬头

2. 哪天咱们请他们去外边撮一顿，怎么样？（　　　）

    A. 我们什么时候请他们去外边吃饭？

    B. 我们找一天请他们去外边吃饭，好不好？

    C. 那天我们去外边吃饭的时候，你怎么了？

    D. 咱们跟他们一起去饭馆儿吃饭，好吗？

3. 你没觉得我做饭的手艺噌噌见长吗？（　　　）

    A. 你应该觉得我做饭的手艺有很大的进步

    B. 我做饭做得跟以前不一样了，你应该知道

    C. 别人都告诉我，我做饭做得比以前好多了

    D. 我做饭做得比以前好多了，对不对？

4. 良师出高徒（　　　）

    A. 好老师教的学生比老师好

    B. 学生学得好不好要看老师教得怎么样

    C. 好学生的老师肯定好

    D. 好老师教的学生也好

5. 我说不饿了，她还真就不让了。（　　　）

    A. 我说不饿了，她就不让我吃饭了

B. 我说不饿了，只是为了客气，可是她也不请我再多吃一点

C. 我说不饿了，她真的听懂了

D. 我说不饿了，她应该问我为什么

6. 在有的方面，中国人比外国人含蓄得多，例如：（　　　）

A. 如果你送一个中国人礼物，他可能会说："你不应该花钱给我买礼物。"

B. 如果你告诉你的中国朋友他英文说得很好，他也许说："还差得很远。"

C. 如果你邀请你的中国朋友吃饭，他可能会说："还是我请你吧。"

D. 上边的三个例子都对。

（三）选择适当的词语，替换句中的画线部分

Choose the most appropriate words to replace the underlined parts

A. 撮一顿　B. 考考你　C. 还真实在　D. 当然了　E. 待会儿见　F. 反正

1. A：你先去吧，我到邮局寄了信就去图书馆找你。

B：好，等一会儿再见。

2. A：谢谢你帮我修好了电脑！哪天你有空我请你出去吃饭。

B：别这么客气了。

3. A：你不是学中文吗？我考你一下吧，这个句子是什么意思？

B：这个句子我还没学过呢！

4. A：这是二十块钱，你多找了我十块钱！

B：我说那十块钱不用给我了，你这个人真诚实！

5. A：你现在做中国饭做得很地道了。

B：哪里哪里，还不行呢。

A：你现在怎么客气起来了？

B：这不奇怪！因为我在中国不但学了中文，还学了中国文化。

6. A：我们英语说得这么不好听，你说麦克会不会笑话我们？

B：不会的，不管怎么样，他知道我们现在正在学英语呢。

（四）用所给词语完成对话

Complete the following dialogues with the items provided in the parenthesis

1. （良师出高徒嘛，当然了，见长）

A：我看你现在打乒乓球的水平_____了。

B：那_____，守着你这么一个好老师，_____。

2. （反正，低头不见抬头见，打招呼）

A：哎，刚走过去的那个人不是你的同屋吗？

B：对！是我同屋。

A：那你怎么不_____呢？

B：我们吵架了，我不想跟他说话。

A：你们两个人住在一起，_____，得好好相处。

B：他现在四年级，_____就要毕业了，再说，我们现在忙得也真没时间说话。

3.（真实在，当然了，撮一顿）

　　A：今天我中文考试全班第一名！

　　B：真的啊！那你得请我去中国饭馆儿_____。

　　A：行啊！去哪家饭馆儿？

　　B：我只是说着玩儿呢，你还_____。

　　A：那_____。

4.（含蓄，真是太香了）

　　A：这儿的饭怎么样？

　　B：_____！我希望你总是考第一名，这样你就可以常请我来这儿吃饭了。

　　A：你倒是不_____！

（五）角色扮演 Role play

Make a dialogue with a classmate. One party plays Mike, and the other Lao Li. Your dialogue should incorporate the provided items.

麦克	老李
You invite Lao Li's family to your house for dinner in return for their hospitality, and to show off your cooking skill. When Mr. Li compliments your cooking skill you thank him for teaching you how to cook.	You gladly accept Mike's invitation. Impressed by Mike's progress with cooking, you compliment him.
1. 邀请 2. 露两手 3. 当然了 4. 良师出高徒	1. 我很高兴接受你的邀请 2. 真地道 3. 手艺见长 4.（不）含蓄

三、课堂讨论 Discussion

1. 你觉得中国人跟邻居打招呼的方式跟你们国家有什么不同？
2. 中国人在哪方面比较含蓄？哪方面不太含蓄？
3. 在你或你熟悉的文化中，人们在哪方面比较含蓄，哪方面不太含蓄？

第七课 朋友，小声点儿

Be Quiet Please

 编剧：万红

人物 (Characters)

胡染 (Hú Rǎn) ——男，二十八岁。

刘安 (Liú Ān) ——男，二十六岁。

周丽 (Zhōu Lì) ——女，三十五岁，某公司部门经理。

课 文 Text

胡　　　染：喂，谁呀？你是谁？你再说一遍——，哎哟，你老兄还活着[N1]呢？你这几年在哪儿**发财**呢？[N2]河南？噢，不是河

---

1. 小声	xiǎoshēng	adv.	(speak) softly; whisper
2. 某	mǒu	pron.	certain; indefinite (person or thing)
3. 部门	bùmén	n.	department; branch; section; division
4. 经理	jīnglǐ	n.	manager
5. 老兄	lǎoxiōng	n.	buddy; pal (colloq.)
6. 发财	fā cái	vo.	get rich; make a fortune
7. 河南	Hénán	N.	Henan (a province in China)

南是**荷兰**，行啊你，**混**得不错啊[N3]——我啊，我**比不了**你，我正**蹦**极呢[N4]，还不知道蹦到什么地方呢。

胡　　染：什么什么？你**大声**一点儿，我**听不见**，我在车上呢……

刘　　安：**哥们**儿，麻烦您**声音**小点儿成吗？您要是有什么话，您一会儿下了车慢慢说。

胡　　染：好了好了好了，噢，对了，我再告诉你一个**手机**号码：13317311121，你下次打这个，哎，好嘞，好嘞好嘞……

刘　　安：**哥们**儿，您能说话小声点儿吗？

胡　　染：我打电话**碍**你什么事[N5]？你**凭**什么不让我说话？

刘　　安：这是公共**场合**，您这么大声说话**影响**大家了……

老年乘客：说得对，他**哇啦哇啦**的大**嗓门**儿**害**得我都没**听见报站名**，**坐过了站**！

8. 荷兰	Hélán	N.	the Netherlands; Holland
9. 混	hùn	v.	(see note 3)
10. 比不了	bǐ bu liǎo	vc.	not comparable to; not as good as
11. 蹦	bèng	v.	jump
12. 大声	dà shēng		loudly; in loud voice
13. 听不见	tīng bu jiàn	vc.	unable to hear; inaudible
14. 哥们儿	gēmenr	n.	buddy; pal (colloq.)
15. 声音	shēngyīn	n.	voice; sound
16. 手机	shǒujī	n.	cell phone
17. 碍	ài	v.	hinder; be in the way of
18. 凭	píng	prep.	with (the authority or quality of)
19. 场合	chǎnghé	n.	site; venue; occasion
20. 影响	yǐngxiǎng		impair; interfere with; affect
21. 老年	lǎonián	n.	(of a person) old; old age
22. 乘客	chéngkè	n.	passenger
23. 哇啦哇啦	wāla wāla		(an onomatopoeia for loud voice)
24. 嗓门儿	sǎngménr	n.	voice
25. 害	hài	v.	impair; cause trouble to
26. 听见	tīng jiàn	vc.	hear
27. 站名	zhànmíng	n.	name of the bus stop or railroad station
28. 坐过了站	zuò guò le zhàn		(of a bus rider) miss the stop

胡　　染：你成心^{N6}起什么哄！你坐过站是你的事，跟我有什么关
　　　　　系？
　　　　（短信：给大家一个宁静与舒心，请勿高声喧哗。一位陌生
　　　　　朋友。）
胡　　染：谁呀？狗拿耗子多管闲事^{N7}！
　　　　（画外音：朝阳门到了，请打开车月票下车！）

应 聘 者：再见。
周　　丽：再见。

29.	成心	chéngxīn	adv.	intentionally; deliberately
30.	起(什么)哄	qǐ (shénme) hòng	vo.	kick up a fuss; stir up a disturbance
31.	关系	guān·xì	n.	relation; relationship; relevance
32.	短信	duǎnxìn	n.	short message (on a cell phone)
33.	宁静	níngjìng	adj.	peaceful and tranquil
34.	与	yǔ	conj.	and (literary)
35.	舒心	shūxīn	adj.	pleasant
36.	请勿	qǐng wù		please do not (literary)
37.	高声	gāo shēng		loud; loudly
38.	喧哗	xuānhuá	v.	make hubbub; make uproar
39.	陌生	mòshēng	adj.	unknown; unfamiliar
40.	耗子	hàozi	n.	mouse; rat
41.	闲事	xiánshì	n.	other people's business
42.	画外音	huà wài yīn	n.	off-screen voice (in film or TV)
43.	朝阳门	Cháoyángmén	N.	(a place in Beijing)
44.	打开	dǎ kāi	vc.	open
45.	月票	yuèpiào	n.	monthly pass (for public transportation)
46.	应聘	yìngpìn	v.	apply (for a job)

秘　　书：这是胡染的资料。

周　　丽：请坐。**恭喜**你**笔试通过**了。今天**复试**我们再**进行**一次**综合测试**。你的条件不错，你的文化专业也和我们的**业务对口**[N8]，你的**技术能力**也和我们的**要求**相**吻合**。可是，

47.	秘书	mìshū	n.	secretary
48.	资料	zīliào	n.	data; information
49.	恭喜	gōngxǐ	v.	congratulate
50.	笔试	bǐshì	n.	written examination
51.	通过	tōngguò	v.	pass; succeed in (an exam; etc.)
52.	复试	fùshì	n.	re-exam; second-round exam
53.	进行	jìnxíng	v.	carry on; carry out; conduct
54.	综合	zōnghé	v.	comprehensive
55.	测试	cèshì	v.	test; assessment
56.	业务	yèwù	n.	vocational work; professional work
57.	对口	duìkǒu	adj.	(see note 8)
58.	技术	jìshù	n.	technology; skill
59.	能力	nénglì	n.	ability; talent
60.	要求	yāoqiú	v.	requirement
61.	吻合	wěnhé	adj.	consistent with

我们公司不仅看重人的聪明才智，我们更看重的是人才素质和人品修养。比如说，公司要求每个员工在任何场所做任何事情都要顾全大局[N9]，不做有损公司形象的事，你说对吗？

胡　　染：说得对。

周　　丽：可是，今天你在公交车上的表现却和我们公司的要求有距离，令人失望，所以能否[N10]录用你，我们再做考虑。

胡　　染：啊？

周　　丽：你看到手机短信了吗？

胡　　染：哦，您就是那位陌生朋友？咳，我真不该这样！经理，

62.	看重	kànzhòng	v.	value; think highly of
63.	聪明	cōngmíng	adj./n.	intelligent, wise; intelligence, wisdom
64.	才智	cáizhì	n.	talent; gift
65.	人才	réncái	n.	person of ability and talent
66.	素质	sùzhì	n.	quality; character
67.	人品	rénpǐn	n.	moral character
68.	修养	xiūyǎng	n.	cultivation
69.	比如说	bǐrú shuō		for example
70.	员工	yuángōng	n.	employee; staff member
71.	任何	rènhé	pron.	any
72.	场所	chǎngsuǒ	n.	place; location; venue
73.	顾全大局	gùquán dàjú		(see note 9)
74.	有损	yǒusǔn	v.	harm; damage
75.	形象	xíngxiàng	n.	image
76.	公交车	gōngjiāochē	n.	vehicle of public transportation
77.	表现	biǎoxiàn	v./n.	behavior; conduct
78.	距离	jùlí	n.	distance; disparity
79.	令人失望	lìng rén shīwàng		disappointing
80.	能否	néng fǒu		possible or not; able or not; whether
81.	录用	lùyòng	v.	employ; hire

您能再给我一次机会吗？

周　丽：机会？机会全得**由**你去**把握**，今天你因小失大^{N11}**失去**了
　　　　一次**竞争**机会，我想，明天还有**许多挑战**在**考验**你，希
　　　　望你能把握**未来**。

胡　染：我**明白**了，**感谢**您的**教诲**。

胡　染：朋友，你也是来应聘的吧？

刘　安：对啊。

胡　染：**兄弟**^{N12}，真的对不起，今天公交车上的事是我错了。

刘　安：咳，过去的就让它过去吧^{N13}，**啥**也别说了。

胡　染：祝你**成功**！

刘　安：谢谢！就让咱们**一切**都从现在开始。

胡　染：好。

82.	机会	jīhuì	n.	opportunity
83.	全	quán	adv.	completely; entirely
84.	由	yóu	prep.	up to (somebody to do something)
85.	把握	bǎwò	n. /v.	grasp; seize
86.	因小失大	yīn xiǎo shī dà		(see note 11)
87.	失去	shīqù	v.	lose; miss
88.	竞争	jìngzhēng	v.	compete
89.	许多	xǔduō	num.	many; much; a lot of
90.	挑战	tiǎozhàn	v. /n.	challenge
91.	考验	kǎoyàn	v. /n.	ordeal; test
92.	未来	wèilái	n.	future
93.	明白	míngbai	v. /adj.	understand; come to see; clear
94.	感谢	gǎnxiè	v.	thank for; be grateful for
95.	教诲	jiàohuì	v.	teaching; instruction; advice
96.	兄弟	xiōngdi	n.	(see note 12)
97.	啥	shá	pron.	what; whatever
98.	成功	chénggōng	v. /n.	succeed; success
99.	一切	yíqiè	pron.	all; everything

注释 Notes

1. "你老兄还活着":

这是很熟的人之间较长时间没有见面，在见面或打电话时的一句开玩笑的话。"老兄"是男人对男人的 一种比较随便的称呼。

"你老兄还活着"（Pal, you're still alive）is formula often used by men to greet each other jokingly, especially after a long period of not seeing each other. "老兄"（pal）is a casual address between men.

2. "你这几年在哪儿发财呢?"

Where have you been making a fortune these years?

这是改革开放有人经商、办企业以后出现的问候语，问话人假定对方是在经商或做赚钱较多的工作。一般用于熟人之间。"发财"是经商、办企业赚了很多钱的意思。

This is a formula of greeting that has become popular since private enterprises started to emerge in China in the 1990s. The speaker assumes the other person to have been engaged in business.

3. "混得不错啊":

"混"本来有"苟且地生活""不是很好地生活"的意思。现在也用来表示一般的"生活"。"混得不错"就是：生活得不错。口语。正式场合不要用。

"混" originally means "to live aimlessly" or "to muddle along". More recently, however, it has come to simply mean "to live". The expression "混得不错" thus means "to lead a decent life" or "to be doing well". It is a colloquialism to be avoided on formal occasions.

（1）A：你毕业好几年了，现在怎么样啊？

　　　　It has been quite a few years since you graduated. How are you doing now?

　　B：混呗，吃饭没问题。

　　　　Just drifting along. It's no problem to feed myself.

（2）他这几年混得不怎么样，工作丢了，老婆也离（婚）了。

　　　He has not been doing well these few years. He lost his job, and was divorced.

(3) 你现在混得不错呀，买了大房子，汽车也开上了。

You are really doing great now：You've bought a big house and are driving a car.

4. "我正蹦极呢"：

"蹦极"是脚被套在绳子里，从很高的地方往下跳的一种很刺激的娱乐活动。这里胡染比喻自己正在找工作。

"蹦极" is a colloquial term for cliff diving. Since it is a very exciting and risky sport，Hu Ran here uses it as a metaphor for job searching. The sentence thus means "I'm looking for a job" or "I'm jumping about on the job market".

5. "碍事"：

"碍事"的意思是"妨碍做事""影响人们活动"。口语。

As a colloquialism，"碍事" means "to hamper other people in their business or activities".

(1) 我打电话，碍你什么事？

I was just making a phone call. What did that have to do with you?

这句话的意思是：我打电话，怎么会妨碍你了？

The sentence suggests "My phone call could not have been disruptive to you".

(2) 这把椅子放在这儿碍事，我出去不方便。

This chair gets in the way. It makes it hard for me to get out.

(3) 孩子在这儿玩儿不碍事，我可以做事。

It's OK for the kids to play here. I can do my work.

"不碍事"还有"不重要""没关系"的意思。

"不碍事" can also mean "It doesn't matter" or "It is of no consequence".

(4) 我刚才摔了一下，只是碰破了一点皮，不碍事。

I fell a moment ago. It was only a bruise，nothing serious.

6. "成心"：

"成心"的意思是故意的，通常用于做不太好的事情。

"成心" means being deliberate or purposeful，usually in an attempt at something bad.

(1) 你成心起什么哄？

How should you try to stir up a disturbance?

（2）您的咖啡洒了，对不起，我不是成心的。

Sorry, your coffee spilled. I was just inadvertent.

（3）这次他考试考得不好，是成心的，他完全没有准备。

He was deliberate in not doing well for this exam. He did not prepare at all.

7. "狗拿耗子多管闲事"：

俗语。"拿"在这里的意思是"抓"。人们认为"抓耗子"是猫应该管的事情。"狗拿耗子多管闲事"用来比喻管自己不该管的的事情（闲事）。

This is a popular saying. The verb "拿" here is interchangeable with "抓" (to catch). As "抓耗子" (to catch rats) is what a cat is supposed to do, "狗拿耗子" (a dog trying to catch a rat) becomes a metaphor for poking one's nose into others' business.

8. "对口"：

"对口"可以表示两方（通常指人和工作或者工作单位之间）在工作内容和性质方面一致。

"对口" may mean the compatibility between one's training and the requirement of a job.

（1）你的文化专业也和我们的业务对口。

Your expertise meets the needs of our business.

这句话的意思是：你学的专业和我们单位的业务一致。"对口"作形容词时，后面不能有宾语，要用"和/跟……对口"。

In this sentence, "对口" is used as an adjective, which means it is not to be followed by an object. It usually appears in the structure "和/跟……对口".

（2）这个工作跟我学的专业不对口，我不想去。

This job has nothing to do with my professional training. I don't want to take it.

（3）你到我们的各个对口单位去了解一下情况。

You go to get some information from the work units in our own field.

9. "顾全大局"：

"顾全"的意思是考虑到、照顾到，"大局"的意思是整个的形势、整体的利益。"顾全大局"的意思就是：照顾整个局面（全局），使之不受损失。相反的意思是：只为个人或者小单位着想，而不管整体利益。

"顾全" means "to pay attention to" or "to give consideration to", and "大局" refers to the overall situation or the interest of the whole. The set phrase "顾全大局" thus means to be thoughtful about the overall situation for the sake of the larger interest. The opposite practice would be to focus on the gain of oneself or the smaller unit to the disregard of the interest of the larger group.

10. **"能否"**:

意思是"能不能"。书面语。

"能否" is a literary equivalent to the more colloquial and more commonly used form "能不能".

11. **"因小失大"**:

意思是：因为小的利益而造成大的损失。

"因小失大" means to suffer a big loss because of a small gain.

(1) 今天你因小失大失去了一次竞争机会，我想，明天还有许多挑战在考验你，希望你能把握未来。

You lost a huge opportunity today because of some trivial things. I think you will be tested by more challenges，and I hope you will be able to handle your future properly.

(2) 你不要因小失大，少赚一点儿钱没关系，但是不要失去别人的信任。

Don't be penny-wise and pound-foolish. It doesn't matter to make a little less money，but you should never lose people's confidence in you.

(3) 这个人为了一点儿小事，打伤了人，不但要给人付医疗费，还差一点儿丢了工作，真是因小失大。

This guy hit and injured someone over a petty dispute. He not only had to pay for all the medical expenses but almost lost his job. It was truly a case of winning small and losing big.

12. **"兄弟"**:

对年纪比自己小的成年男子的称呼。口语。

"兄弟" can serve as a colloquial address for a male adult younger than oneself.

13. **"过去的就让它过去吧"**

Let what is gone be gone.

当刚刚过去或已经过去的事会使人伤心、痛苦、悔恨时，说这句话的意思是：忘记不愉快的过去吧。

What is suggested by the sentence is：If the past was unpleasant，let's try to forget it.

听说练习　Listening & Speaking Exercises

■ 一、课文理解 Text Comprehension

（一）根据故事情节选择适当的答案

Please choose the most appropriate answer based on the story

1. 胡染在哪儿打电话呢？（　　）

　　A. 荷兰　　　　　　　B. 河南　　　　　　　C. 公共汽车上

2. 大家对胡染都很不高兴，因为（　　）

　　A. 他混得不错　　　B. 多管闲事　　　C. 高声喧哗

3. 一位老年乘客因为胡染说话声音太大（　　）

　　A. 坐过了站　　　　B. 哇啦哇啦　　　C. 跟着起哄

4. 胡染现在（　　）

　　A. 在车上蹦极呢　　B. 发财了　　　C. 正在找工作

5. 胡染说谁"狗拿耗子多管闲事"？（　　）

　　A. 起哄的人

　　B. 发短信的人

　　C. 坐过了站的人

6. 周丽的公司非常看重人的（　　）

　　A. 素质和修养

　　B. 技术能力

　　C. 聪明才智

7. 胡染没被录用，因为（　　）

　　A. 素质和修养不够

　　B. 笔试没通过

　　C. 专业和公司的业务不对口

8. 给胡染手机发短信的是（　　）

A．陌生朋友　　　　B．刘安　　　　C．周丽

（二）根据课文判断下面句子意思的正误

State whether the following statements are true or false based on the story

1.（　）胡染和刘安都在找工作。
2.（　）给胡染打电话的人这几年在河南工作。
3.（　）胡染认为给他发短信的人是成心起哄。
4.（　）老年乘客因为胡染大嗓门儿坐过了站。
5.（　）胡染说刘安要他安静是"狗拿耗子多管闲事"。
6.（　）胡染没被立刻录用是因为他对周丽很不客气。
7.（　）虽然胡染没被立刻录用，但是他对周丽的教诲很感谢。
8.（　）周丽怕胡染会做有损公司形象的事，所以不愿意立刻录用他。

（三）先听故事叙述，然后复述故事

Listen to the narrative first and then retell the story

　　胡染坐公共汽车去应聘工作。他在车上时有人给他打电话，原来是个几年没见的老朋友，他就高兴地跟他聊起来。他说话的声音太大，一位乘客请他小声点儿，他不但不听，反而很不客气地说他打电话不碍谁的事，谁也不能不让他说话。车上的人都很不高兴。一位老年乘客还因他声音太大而坐过了站。这时胡染接到一个手机短信，请他不要高声喧哗，他却认为这个人是"狗拿耗子多管闲事"。

　　到了应聘的公司。接见他的周丽告诉他虽然他的条件不错，专业和公司的业务对口，技术能力也和公司的要求相吻合，但是他们不能录用他。原来，周丽就是给他发短信的那位陌生朋友。周丽还说他们公司不仅看重人的聪明才智，更看重人才素质和人品修养，而胡染在公交车上的表现和公司的要求有距离，令她很失望，所以公司是否录用胡染，他们要再做考虑。胡染认识到了自己的错误，很感谢周丽的教诲。

■ 二、词语使用 Application of Vocabulary and Grammar

（一）选择题

Choose the item that is grammatically correct

1. 哎呀，你老兄还活着呢？你这几年＿＿＿＿＿＿发财呢？
　　A．跟谁　　　B．有多少　　　C．在哪儿　　　D．怎么

2. 我打电话碍你什么事？你＿＿＿＿＿＿不让我说话？
　　A．麻烦我　　　B．不能　　　C．凭什么　　　D．不讲理

3. 你坐_____站是你的事，跟我有什么关系？

    A. 过   B. 了

    C. 忘   D. 去

4. 今天你在公交车上的表现却和我们公司的要求有_____，令人失望，所以我们不能录用你。

    A. 距离   B. 问题

    C. 不一样   D. 不同

（二）选择题

Circle the answer that best reflects the meaning of the underlined portion of the sentence

1. 你<u>成心</u>起什么哄啊！（　　　）

    A. 坏心

    B. 有心

    C. 故意

    D. 小心

2. 我们公司<u>不仅看重人的聪明才智，我们更看重的是人才素质和人品修养</u>。（　　　）

    A. 聪明才智不重要了

    B. 人才素质和人品修养最重要

    C. 人才素质比人品修养重要

    D. 人才素质和人品修养比聪明才智更重要

3. 哎呀，<u>你老兄还活着呢</u>？你这几年在哪儿发财呢？（　　　）

    A. 好久没联系了

    B. 你大哥还活着呢

    C. 没想到你还没死

    D. 很高兴你还活着

4. 今天你失去了一次竞争机会，我想，<u>明天</u>还有许多挑战在考验你，希望你能把握未来。（　　　）

    A. 第二天

    B. 以后

    C. 将来

    D. 未来

5. 过去的就让它过去吧，啥也别说了。（　　）

    A. 谁

    B. 怎么

    C. 什么

    D. 干吗

（三）用所给词语完成对话

Complete the following dialogues with the items provided in the parenthesis

1.（麻烦您……，凭什么）

    甲：喂，谁呀？你大声一点儿，我听不见，哎呀，是你老兄啊！最近混得怎么样？

    乙：哥们儿，_____声音小点儿成吗？有什么话，一会儿下了车慢慢说。

    甲：我打电话碍你什么事？你_____不让我说话？

2.（请勿，成心）

    甲：你哇啦哇啦的大嗓门儿害得我都没听见报站名，坐过了站！

    乙：你这是_____起哄！你坐过站是你的事，跟我有什么关系？

    丙：这是公共场合，_____高声喧哗。

    乙：你别"狗拿耗子多管闲事"！

3.（因小失大，感谢，顾全大局）

    甲：公司要求每个员工在任何场所做任何事情都要_____，不做有损公司形象的事。

    乙：你说得对。

    甲：今天你_____失去了一次竞争机会，但是明天还有许多挑战在考验你，希望你能把握未来。

    乙：我明白了，_____您的教诲。

4.（哥们儿，兄弟）

    甲：_____，麻烦您声音小点儿成吗？

    乙：我声音大小碍你什么事？

    甲：你声音太大我没听见报站名，坐过了站了，你知道不知道？

    乙：是吗？哎呀！_____，真的对不起，我这就关机。

（四）角色扮演 Role play

Make a dialogue with a classmate. One party plays Hu Ran, and the other plays Liu An. Your dialogue should incorporate the provided items.

胡染	周丽
You arrived at the company for a job interview. You are pleased to hear that you have passed the written test and your qualifications also meet the job description. However，you are not chosen for the position because of what happened on the bus today. You apologize for your behavior and ask for another chance to improve yourself. At the end，you tell your interviewer that you understand the situation and thank her for the valuable lesson she has taught you.	You congratulate Hu Ran for having passed the written test and tell him that his qualifications also meet the job description. However，you inform him that he is not to be chosen for the position because of what happened on the bus today. You explain to him that the company values a person's integrity and moral character more than his talent and skill. You are also very disappointed by his selfish behavior on the bus which would be very damaging to the company's public image if he were an employee. You encourage Hu Ran to learn from this experience and handle future challenges better.
1. 说得对 2. 您就是…… 3. 我真不该…… 4. 再给我一次机会 5. 明白 6. 感谢 7. 教诲	1. 综合测试　　2. 对口 3. 相吻合　　4. 聪明才智 5. 人才素质　　6. 人品修养 7. 顾全大局　　8. 有损…… 9. 令人失望　　10. 竞争机会 11. 考验

三、课堂讨论 Discussion

1. 你对胡染的行为有什么看法？
2. 要是你在胡染乘坐的车上，你会怎么做？
3. 胡染的条件很好，周丽为什么没有立刻录用他？
4. 要是你是周丽，你会作出跟她一样的决定吗？

第八课 假 币

Counterfeit Money

编 剧：尤欣

人物 （Characters）

王大爷（Wáng dàye）

王大爷的儿子 （Wáng dàye de érzi）

王大爷的老伴儿 （Wáng dàye de lǎobànr）

肉铺老板 （ròupù lǎobǎn）

课 文 Text

老　板：怎么着，大爷，来^{N1}点儿什么您？

王大爷：来二斤猪肉！

老　板：二斤猪肉，好嘞。二斤猪肉，九块，来，给您。

王大爷：放心吧，**假不了**。

---

1. 假币	jiǎbì	n.	fake money; counterfeit
2. 肉铺	ròupù	n.	meat shop
3. 老板	lǎobǎn	n.	boss; manager; shopkeeper
4. 斤	jīn	m.	of weight (equal to 1/2 kilogram)
5. 猪肉	zhūròu	n.	pork
6. 假不了	jiǎ bu liǎo	vc.	cannot be fake

老　板：还是**仔细**点儿好，找您九十一，这是五十的，您拿好啊。

王大爷：那什么，你忙着啊。

老　伴：**老头子**，这张五十的怎么像**假**的呀？你看看。

王大爷：不会吧，哎呀，还真是假的。

王大爷：小伙子。

老　板：**老爷子**，还来点儿什么？来点儿排骨？

王大爷：刚才你找我的五十块钱是假的，麻烦你给我换一张。

老　板：凭什么说这张假币是我找给您的？您这么**大岁数**，可别随便冤枉人！

王大爷：小伙子，你**年纪轻轻**的，记性这么不好啊——刚才我在你这儿买的二斤猪肉，你**这会**儿就忘了？

7. 仔细	zǐxì	adj.	careful; cautious
8. 老头子	lǎotóuzi	n.	old man, husband(wife's term of address for her old husband)
9. 假	jiǎ	adj.	fake; false
10. 老爷子	lǎoyézi	n.	old man; elderly person
11. 岁数	suìshu	n.	age
12. 年纪轻	niánjì qīng		young
13. 这会儿	zhè huìr		now; at the moment

老　板：说我找给您的假币，有证据吗？没有，赶紧走，别**耽误**我
　　　　做生意。

小　王：爸，谁给您的**假钱**？

王大爷：就是**市场**头一家卖肉的！

小　王：这样，你把那假钱给我，我有办法……

王大爷：你能有什么办法？

小　王：行了，行了，您就甭管了，**瞧好**儿**吧**[N2]您啊！

小　王：**怎么卖**的？

老　板：猪肉四块五，排骨六块。

小　王：给我来一斤猪肉、三斤排骨。

老　板：得，一斤猪肉是吧，三斤排骨。

小　王：行了，甭算了，二斤猪肉九块钱，三斤排骨十八块钱，**加
　　　　起来**一共是二十七，没错吧？给您五十。

老　板：找您二十三，二十……三块。

小　王：谢谢您了。

王大爷：不可能吧？那个老板那么仔细，能把那假钱收了？

14.	证据	zhèngjù	n.	evidence; proof
15.	耽误	dānwu	v.	delay; make worse because of delay
16.	做生意	zuò shēngyi	vo.	do business
17.	假钱	jiǎ qián		fake money
18.	市场	shìchǎng	n.	market; marketplace
19.	瞧好儿吧	qiáo hǎor bā		(see note 2)
20.	怎么卖	zěnme mài		How much?
21.	加起来	jiā qilai	vc.	total; add together

小　王：我呀，**先假装算错账，故意**多给他一斤猪肉钱。他呢，肯定怕我**反应过来，巴不得**[N3]赶紧找我钱让我**走人**。您说，这时候他还能分清这个钱是真的假的吗？

王大爷：人人都像你们这样，那假钱不是满天飞了吗？[N4]不行，我还得去一**趟**。

老　板：看见没有，又收了张假币，我还不知道找谁**说理**去呢。**嗨**，我正找你呢。

王大爷：哎呀，你怎么也来了，回去吧。

小　王：您甭管，这事您甭管，您甭管了。

老　板：你给了我一张假币，走，到**市场管理处**说理去！

小　王：好啊，我正要和你一起去呢。爸，**正好**把这个假钱跟他**说道说道**[N5]！

老　板：你们俩是一家的？

小　王：我告诉你，就是你刚才给我爸的，走吧，市场管理处，走，走，走。

22. 假装	jiǎzhuāng	v.	pretend
23. 算错账	suàn cuò zhàng		add the sum wrong
24. 故意	gùyì	adv.	intentionally；deliberately
25. 反应过来	fǎnyìng guolai	vc.	realize
26. 巴不得	bābude	v.	cannot wait（to do sth.）；be anxious（to do sth.）
27. 走人	zǒu rén	vo.	leave
28. 趟	tàng	m.	（measure word for a trip）
29. 说理	shuō lǐ	vo.	argue；dispute
30. 嗨	hēi	interj.	（used to call attention）hey
31. 市场管理处	shìchǎng guǎnlǐchù		Market Management Department
32. 正好	zhènghǎo	adv.	coincidentally
33. 说道	shuōdao	v.	discuss

王大爷：行了，行了^{N6}，行了！

老　板：您看，这是怎么话_儿说的^{N7}呢，我这一天做小买卖，也挣不
　　　　了几个钱^{N8}，还收了张假币。

王大爷：你上当了，就别让更多人也上当啊，对不对啊？

老　板：都是我的不对，您二位就别跟我计较^{N9}了。

王大爷：其实我今天来啊就是说清楚这个事。当然了，我儿子做得
　　　　也不对。收了假币都像你们这样，到头来^{N10}吃亏的是自
　　　　己。这昧良心的事_儿不能干，今天这个事就是个教训。

老　板：大爷，您说得太对了，这昧良心的事_儿咱不能干。

王大爷：这张假币，尽快上缴银行吧……

34.	做小买卖	zuò xiǎo mǎimai	vo.	do small business; do little trading
35.	上当	shàng dàng	vo.	be fooled
36.	计较	jìjiào	v.	discuss in minute detail; argue; dispute
37.	说清楚	shuō qīngchu	vc.	make clear; state clearly
38.	吃亏	chī kuī	vo.	suffer losses
39.	昧良心	mèi liángxīn	vo.	go against one's conscience
40.	教训	jiàoxun	v.	lesson
41.	尽快	jǐnkuài	adv.	as quickly (soon) as possible
42.	上缴	shàngjiǎo	v.	turn over (to a higher authority)

注释 Notes

1. **"来":**

"来" 可以表示做某个动作，这时它可以代替其他动词，可用于买东西（代替 "买"）、在饭馆儿点菜（代替 "要" "点"）等等。口语。

"来" can be used to replace a specific verb when its meaning is understood by both the speaker and the listener. For instance，in "我来!" （"Let me do it"），or "小李来一个" （"Xiao Li （should） perform"），since the specific action is known to the listener，the speaker can simply use "来" instead of mentioning the specific verb. "来" is frequently used when ordering food in a restaurant，or making a purchase in a store. It is a colloquial expression.

(1) 怎么着，大爷，来点儿什么您？

What can I do for you，Daye，What do you want？

(2) 服务员，再来一碗米饭。

Excuse me，one bowl of rice please.

(3) （一位男士看见一位女同事在搬东西）我来，我来！

Here，here，I'll do it！

(4) （很多人在一起，请一个人表演）小李来一个！

Come on，Xiao Li！

2. **"瞧好儿吧":**

相信事情会有好的结果时可以这样对别人说。口语。

"瞧好吧"，a colloquial expression，is used when the speaker believes that a desired outcome or result will definitely occur.

(1) 王大爷：你能有什么办法？

Wang daye：What can you do about it？

小王：行了，行了，您就甭管了。瞧好儿吧您啊！

Xiao Wang：It's fine，you don't have to worry about it. Just wait and see.

(2) A：这场比赛咱们队能赢吗？

Can our team win this match？

B：肯定能赢，你就瞧好儿吧。

Of course，just watch.

3. **"巴不得"**：

意思是：很迫切地希望。口语。

"巴不得"，a colloquial expression，means "cannot wait to（do st.）；anxious to（do st.）".

（1）我先假装算错账，故意多给他一斤猪肉钱。他呢，肯定怕我反应过来，巴不得赶紧找我钱让我走人，……

First I pretended to total the bill wrong by giving him an extra *jin* of pork's worth of money. He must have been afraid that I would realize my "mistake", so he hurriedly gave me my change and got rid of me.

（2）快放假了，他巴不得马上就回家。

Soon will be vacation time，and he can't wait to go home.

（3）他下周要考试，女朋友打电话说周末可能不来了。他巴不得女朋友不来，忙说："好好。"

He's going to have a test next week，and his girlfriend called to tell him that she might not be able to come this weekend. This is truly what he had wished to happen；so he agreed quickly and eagerly.

4. **"那假钱不是满天飞了吗?"**：

"满天飞"这里比喻到处都有。再如"谣言满天飞"。也可以比喻一个人到处乱跑。如：小李一天到晚满天飞，打手机都找不到他。

"满天飞" means "everywhere". For example，one can say "谣言满天飞"，meaning "the rumor was spread everywhere". Another example，"小李一天到晚满天飞" indicates that "小李" travels everywhere from morning until dark.

5. **"说道说道"**：

"说道说道"这里的意思是用语言表达出来，和"说说"意思差不多，但更加口语。

"说道说道" emphasizes verbal expression. It is similar to "说说"，except that it is more colloquial.

（1）好啊，我正要和你一起去呢。爸，正好把这个假钱和他说道说道！

Sure，I was just about to go with you. Dad，now we can discuss the issue of the counterfeit money with him.

（2）小李，你把刚才跟我说的意思跟大家说道说道。

Xiao Li，tell everyone what you just said to me.

（3）我想把我的想法跟大家说道说道，你们有时间听吗？

I'd like to tell everyone my opinion on this issue. Do you have time?

6. **"行了，行了"**:

"行"有"可以"的意思。"行了，行了"往往用来阻止别人说话或做事。这样说时，可能因为急于做其他事或者不耐烦，所以不是很客气。口语。

"行"，a colloquial expression, is similar to "可以"（"ok"）. However, by using "行了，行了"（"Okay, okay!"）, the speaker often intends to stop the listening from saying/doing something that the speaker does not approve of, and would like to change the topic. This expression reflects the speaker's impatience, and can be rude.

（1）王大爷：你能有什么办法？

Wang Daye：what can you do about it?

小王：行了，行了，您就甭管了。瞧好儿吧，您啊！

Xiao Wang：Please don't worry. You just wait and see!

（2）小李：我跟你说了这么长时间，你答应不答应？

Xiao Li：I've talked to you for so long, but is it okay with you or not?

小张：行了行了，我答应你就是了。

Xiao Zhang：Okay, okay, [shut up.] I'll do it.

（3）行了行了，别写了，我们该走了。

Please! Don't write any more, the class is over.

7. **"这是怎么话儿说的"**:

意思是：事情怎么会这样？说话人往往因为对事情做得不好，有责任，所以包含一定歉意。年轻人较少这样说。口语。

"这是怎么话说的"，a colloquial expression, is used mostly by elderly people. It means "how did things become this way?" The speaker usually indicates some sort of apology for being responsible for a mistake or error.

（1）您看，这是怎么话儿说的。我这一天做小买卖，也挣不了几个钱，还收了张假币。

Look at this! How can this be? I worked a whole day selling small trinkets on the streets, not earning much, and yet someone has given me a fake bill.

（2）孙女：奶奶，你看，你把我的作业本弄湿了。

Granddaughter：Grandma, look, you got my workbook wet.

奶奶：这是怎么话说的，我给你擦擦。

Grandma：How did this happen? Let me wipe it for you.

8. **"挣不了几个钱"**:

这里的"几个"表示"很少"的意思。口语。

"几个", a colloquial term, meaning very little, or very few.

(1) 我这一天做小买卖，也挣不了几个钱，……

I don't make much money doing a little business like this.

(2) 周末校园里没有几个人，很安静。

There aren't many people on campus at weekends, so it's very quiet.

(3) 他就那么几本中文书，你要看的书他没有。

He has just a few Chinese books, and doesn't have the one you want to read.

9. **"计较"**:

"计较"有争论的意思。

"计较" means to bicker or to dispute.

(1) 都是我的不对，您二位就别跟我计较了。

I know this is all my fault. Would you two please stop arguing with me.

(2) 好了好了，别说了，我不跟你计较了。

Okay, it's enough. I'm not arguing with you any more.

"计较"还有"过分计算个人得失"的意思。

"计较" can also means that someone is too particular about money or trifles.

(1) 他这个人在钱的方面很计较。

He is really stingy with money.

(2) 跟别人相处不要斤斤计较，对人要宽厚一些。

Don't be so particular about trivial matters, be more generous to people.

10. **"到头来"**:

"到头来"的意思是：到最后，结果。多用于不好的事情。口语。

"到头来", a colloquial expression, meaning "in the end". It is more often than not used to indicate some bad result, or negative outcome.

(1) 收了假币都像你们这样，到头来吃亏的是自己。

If you receive counterfeit money and deal with it like you did before, you would victimize yourself in the end.

（2）他跟朋友总是斤斤计较，到头来朋友们都离开了他。

He was always very petty with his friends, and in the end they all left him.

（3）你是学生，可是不上课，不做作业，到头来非被学校开除不可。

You're a student, but you don't go to class, nor do your homework. You will definitely end up being expelled by the school.

听说练习　Listening & Speaking Exercises

■ 一、课文理解 Text Comprehension

（一）根据故事情节选择适当的答案

Please choose the most appropriate answer based on the story

1. 王大爷买了二斤猪肉花了（　　）

    A. 五十块钱　　　　　B. 九块钱　　　　　C. 九十一块钱

2. 卖肉的老板找王大爷钱的时候（　　）

    A. 知道那张五十块钱是假的

    B. 不知道那张五十块钱是假的

    C. 怀疑那张五十块钱是假的

3. 王大爷回去找老板的时候（　　）

    A. 老板不记得王大爷了

    B. 老板忙得没有时间跟他说话

    C. 老板假装不记得王大爷了

4. 王大爷的儿子小王又去了肉店，因为他要（　　）

    A. 想办法把假钱退还给老板

    B. 再买一些肉和排骨

    C. 跟老板把假币的事说道说道

5. 老板收了假币，因为他（　　）

    A. 以为小王算错账，让自己多赚钱了

    B. 承认自己做错了

    C. 担心小王去找市场管理处

6. 小王能把假币退还给老板，是因为他（　　）

    A. 知道老板会认错

    B. 知道老板有一点儿怕市场管理处

    C. 知道老板只想多赚钱

7. 王大爷第二次去肉店，因为他要（　　）

    A. 让老板承认错误

    B. 把假币的事说清楚

    C. 告诉老板他上当了

8. 最后老板（　　）

    A. 没有挣什么钱　　　B. 认错了　　　　　C. 吃亏了

（二）根据课文判断下面句子意思的正误

State whether the following statements are true or false based on the story

1. （　　）王大爷买肉的时候被卖肉的老板骗了。

2. （　　）卖肉的老板不知道那五十块钱是假币。

3. （　　）小王去找老板说理了。

4. （　　）老板收了小王给的五十块钱假币。

5. （　　）小王很明白老板心里想什么。

6. （　　）王大爷觉得他的儿子很聪明。

7. （　　）王大爷担心市场管理处来找他的儿子。

8. （　　）假钱应该交到银行。

（三）先听故事叙述，然后复述故事

Listen to the narrative first and then retell the story

    王大爷去买肉的时候，卖肉的老板找了他一张五十块钱的假币。他发现以后回去找老板换钱，但是老板假装不认识他。王大爷的儿子小王，知道了以后很生气。他用了一个很聪明的办法把假钱还给了老板。

    王大爷知道了以后很着急。他担心这样下去，更多的人会吃亏。他找到卖肉的老板，把假钱的事说清楚了。

    通过这件事，大家都认识到：昧良心的事情绝对不能做！

二、词语使用 Application of Vocabulary and Grammar

（一）选择题

Choose the item that is grammatically correct

1. 对不起，我这儿有二十块钱，能不能_____您给我换两张十块的？

    A. 让　　　B. 问　　　C. 麻烦　　　D. 耽搁

2. 我没拿你的iPod，我连见都没见过你的iPod，你可别_____怀疑人。

    A. 随便　　　B. 顺便　　　C. 方便　　　D. 特地

3. 我的同屋告诉我他下个学期要搬出去了。我真_____他赶紧走。

他每天打电话吵得我没有办法学习。

    A. 耽误   B. 巴不得   C. 说理   D. 甭管

4. 那家电脑修理店不但没修好我的电脑，还比别人多收了五十块钱，我应该找他们_____。

    A. 收钱   B. 说道说道   C. 计较   D. 说理

5. 卖肉的老板以为他多收了小王的钱，_____他收了一张假币。

    A. 当然   B. 还是   C. 瞧好吧   D. 其实

（二）选择题

Circle the answer that best reflects the meaning of the sentence

1. 我还是仔细点儿好。（   ）

    A. 虽然我不相信你，可是我还是应该放心

    B. 虽然我相信你，可是我还是得小心一点儿

    C. 虽然我认识你，可是我还是得麻烦一点儿

    D. 虽然我认识你，可是我不能吃亏

2. 您这么大岁数，可别随便冤枉人啊！（   ）

    A. 您老了，记性不好了，但是不能怀疑别人

    B. 虽然我们应该对老人客气，但是老人不应该不尊敬别人

    C. 您岁数大，经验多，不应该这样不负责任地怀疑别人

    D. 老人可能记性不好了，但是对别人应该很好

3. 我刚找了你二十块钱，你这会儿就忘了？（   ）

    A. 我刚找了你二十块钱，你会忘吗？

    B. 我刚找了你二十块钱，你这么快就忘了吗？

    C. 我刚找了你二十块钱，你不会忘吧？

    D. 我刚找了你二十块钱，我想你没忘。

4. 那个老板那么仔细，能把那假钱给收了？（   ）

    A. 那个老板这么年纪轻轻，怎么分不清钱是真的还是假的？

    B. 那个老板这么聪明，他怎么能相信你？

    C. 那个老板这么认真，难道他愿意吃亏吗？

    D. 那个老板这么小心，难道他要了你给他的假钱？

5. 因为他在钱的方面比较计较，所以总跟女朋友相处不好。（   ）

    A. 因为他比较在乎钱，所以总跟女朋友相处得不好

    B. 因为他比较会算账，所以总跟女朋友相处得不错

C. 因为他常说钱，所以总跟女朋友相处不好

D. 因为他不在乎钱，所以总跟女朋友相处不好

6. 你上当了，就别让更多的人也上当啊！（　　）

　　A. 既然你被别人骗了，就应该别让更多的人再被骗

　　B. 如果你吃亏了，你就应该帮助别人赚钱

　　C. 要是你被别人骗了，你应该告诉大家这件事

　　D. 虽然你吃亏了，可是你也不应该骗别人

（三）选择适当的词语，改写句中的画线部分

Choose the most appropriate words to replace the underlined parts

A. 其实	B. 到头来	C. 甭	D. 来
E. 计较钱	F. 巴不得	G. 还是……好	H. 麻烦你

1. 听说这个饭馆儿的排骨做得很好吃，我们<u>点</u>一个吧。

2. A：你想吃素饺子还是肉饺子？

　　B：我这两天肚子不太舒服，<u>最好吃素</u>一点的。

3. 他跟女朋友出去吃饭的时候总是算账算得很清楚，<u>最后</u>，他交了五年的女朋友跟他分手了。

4. "妈，<u>别</u>老给我打电话了，我的同学都笑话我不独立了。"

5. 上中学的时候，我<u>真希望</u>早点儿离开家，现在，我离家远了，反而常常想家。

6. "你去图书馆吗？<u>不好意思</u>，请你帮我把这本书还给图书馆，行吗？"

7. 老李说："吃了吗？"麦克以为老李请他吃饭，<u>可是</u>，他不知道，老李只是跟他打招呼。

（四）用所给词语完成对话

Complete the following dialogues with the items provided in the parenthesis

1. （其实，冤枉，假装）

　　A：那个小伙子还没还你钱吗？我看，他是　　　　　　　忘记这件事，　　　　　　　是不想还给你钱了。

　　B：你别　　　　　　　人家，我知道，他是个讲信誉的人。

2. （巴不得，这会儿）

　　A：我们的飞机马上就要到北京了！

　　B：我现在觉得好紧张。

　　A：上飞机的时候还　　　　　　　一下子就到北京，怎么　　　　　　　倒紧张起来了？

3.（其实，行了行了，假装，到头来）

A：_____，很多人说外语的时候都紧张，说不紧张的人也是_____不紧张。可是，越紧张就越说错，_____，就不喜欢说外语了。

B：_____，别说了，我们已经到北京了。准备下飞机吧！

4.（麻烦，当然）

A：对不起，可以_____你帮我把那本书拿下来吗？

B：_____可以。

（五）角色扮演 Role play

Make a dialogue with a classmate. One person plays Uncle Wang，and the other plays the butcher. Your dialogue should incorporate the provided items.

王大爷	卖肉的老板
You found that the 50 *yuan* the meat seller just gave you is a counterfeit bill. You go back and talk to him. But he denied ever having anything to do with this，so you threaten to take him to the Office of Market Management.	You thought you had got rid of the counterfeit bill of 50 *yuan*（by giving it to an elderly man as change），but the old man came back demanding an exchange. Pretend that you don't remember him and that you are clueless about this counterfeit bill.
1. 假的 2. 麻烦 3. 换 4. 刚才……，这会儿就…… 5. 市场管理处	1. 这么大岁数 2. 冤枉 3. 凭什么…… 4. 耽误

三、课堂讨论 Discussion

1. 如果你是王大爷，发现自己上当了，你会怎么做？

2. 王大爷的儿子为什么不跟卖肉的老板说理，而是用别的办法？

3. 你认为王大爷儿子的办法好吗？为什么？

第九课 责 任

Responsibility

 编剧：夏有志

人物（Characters）

滕超（Téng Chāo）——男青年。
吕青（Lǚ Qīng）——滕超的女朋友。

课 文 Text

吕　青：我喜欢**欧式家具**，欧式家具**体现**着**时尚**，有**格调**有**品位**，你想想，要是在一个**布满**欧式家具的房间里听着**博拉姆斯**

---

1. 责任	zérèn	n.	responsibility
2. 青年	qīngnián	n.	youth; young person
3. 欧式	ōushì	adj.	of European style
4. 家具	jiājù	n.	furniture
5. 体现	tǐxiàn	v.	embody; reflect
6. 时尚	shíshàng	n.	fashion; vogue
7. 格调	gédiào	n.	style
8. 品位	pǐnwèi	n.	rank; grade; status
9. 布满	bùmǎn	vc.	be covered by
10. 博拉姆斯	Bólāmǔsī	N.	Johannes Brahms (19th-century German composer)

的**小夜曲**，多浪漫啊……哎，你看那是什么呀？

滕　超：哟，这是哪个**大款**啊，这么好的一个**手包**就**淘汰**了。

吕　青：不会吧，我看看。

滕　超：看什么呀，连**钢蹦**儿都没有。不对吧，这手包肯定有问题。

吕　青：怎么了？你可别吓我啊。

滕　超：你想想，手包里一分钱都没有，**说明**什么？

吕　青：说明什么？

滕　超：肯定是**小偷**儿在第一现场偷了这个包，**拿走**了手包里的钱、手机等**值钱**的东西，然后来到这个**偏僻**的地方，**将**手包**扔**在这里。这肯定是第二现场。

吕　青：有**道理**！行啊，没想到你还有这**两下子**[N1]，**福尔摩斯**先生。

11.	小夜曲	xiǎoyèqǔ	n.	serenade
12.	大款	dàkuǎn	n.	person of wealth (colloq.)
13.	手包	shǒubāo	n.	handbag; purse
14.	淘汰	táotài	v.	eliminate through selection; discard
15.	钢蹦儿	gāngbèngr	n.	coin (colloq.)
16.	说明	shuōmíng	v.	denote; demonstrate
17.	小偷儿	xiǎotōur	n.	petty thief
18.	现场	xiànchǎng	n.	scene (of event or incident); site; spot
19.	拿走	ná zǒu	vc.	take away
20.	值钱	zhíqián	adj.	valuable
21.	偏僻	piānpì	adj.	remote; out of the way
22.	将	jiāng	prep.	(a more formal equivalent of the preposition 把)
23.	扔	rēng	v.	throw; throw away
24.	道理	dào·lǐ	n.	truth; reason
25.	两下子	liǎng xiàzi		(see note 1)
26.	福尔摩斯	Fú'ěrmósī	N.	Sherlock Holmes (a detective in the works of the 19th-century English novelist Arthur Conan Doyle)

滕　超：咱们走吧，**此地**不可久留[N2]。
吕　青：那里**好像**还有别的什么吧？[N3]

滕　超：好像还有两张**纸**……
吕　青：两张纸？
吕　青：**电汇收据，二十万**呢！有**名片**！我们马上就可以找到
　　　　失主了！
滕　超：你怎么不想想**后果**？[N4]
吕　青：什么后果啊？

27.	此地	cǐ dì		this place; here.
28.	好像	hǎoxiàng	v.	seem like
29.	纸	zhǐ	n.	paper
30.	电汇	diànhuì	v.	transfer money telegraphically
31.	收据	shōujù	n.	receipt
32.	二十万	èrshí wàn	num.	two hundred thousand
33.	名片	míngpiàn	n.	business card
34.	失主	shīzhǔ	n.	owner (of the lost item)
35.	后果	hòuguǒ	n.	consequence

滕　超：多一事不如少一事[N5]你懂吗？你把它交给**警察**，**也许**警察能找到失主，可到时候咱们麻烦就大了！

吕　青：咱们会有什么麻烦？

滕　超：你也不想想，你把**合同**和**汇款**收据给交了，到时候人家就会问手包里的钱呢？手机呢？**卡**呢？

吕　青：可是咱们**根本**没看见那些东西啊！

滕　超：你说你没看见，谁**作证**啊？人家会信吗？人家就不会**相信**咱们把钱给**昧**了？

吕　青：可咱们**确实**没有啊！

滕　超：你也太**天真**了吧你！失主是谁？是个什么样的人？你知道吗？到时候失主**愣**说手袋里有一千块钱，有**一万**块钱，要是再说卡里有**一百万**，你怎么办？

吕　青：失主会吗？

36.	不如	bùrú	v.	not as good as
37.	警察	jǐngchá	n.	police
38.	也许	yěxǔ	adv.	perhaps; probably; maybe
39.	合同	hétong	n.	agreement; contract
40.	汇款	huìkuǎn	v. /n.	remittance
41.	卡	kǎ	n.	card; credit card
42.	根本	gēnběn	adv.	absolutely; fundamentally
43.	作证	zuò zhèng	vo.	testify; serve as witness
44.	相信	xiāngxìn	v.	believe
45.	昧	mèi	v.	conceal
46.	确实	quèshí	adv.	indeed; truly
47.	天真	tiānzhēn	adj.	naïve
48.	愣	lèng	adv.	insist on
49.	一万	yíwàn	num.	ten thousand
50.	一百万	yìbǎiwàn	num.	a million

滕　超：好，咱再**退一步说**[N6]，就算失主不会，可这也是个**刑事案件**啊，到时候警察三天一**调查**，五天一**取证**[N7]，你就甭想**消停**了！

吕　青：可是……

滕　超：别那么多可是可是了，咱们还是别多这个事儿了。

吕　青：可是，你怎么就**单单**没有考虑到那个手袋的失主会**遇到**什么麻烦呢？那个合同和**汇票对于他来说**[N8]也许很重要呢？我们是有可能遇到麻烦，但是，有失主的麻烦大吗？

滕　超：咱们玩儿得好好的，你干吗**非要**多这个事儿[N9]啊？

吕　青：不是我想**多事**，如果我们没有看到，那和我们没有关系；但是**既然**看到了，我就觉得我们有这个责任。

滕　超：哎哟，**姑奶奶**，**荒郊野外**的，哪儿来的责任啊？责任，**这哪**儿**跟哪**儿啊[N10]，谁给咱责任啦？

51.	退一步说	tuì yí bù shuō		（see note 6）
52.	刑事	xíngshì	adj.	criminal
53.	案件	ànjiàn	n.	law suit; case
54.	调查	diàochá	v.	investigate
55.	取证	qǔ zhèng	vo.	collect evidence
56.	消停	xiāoting	adj.	calm; uneventful
57.	单单	dāndān	adv.	only; solely
58.	遇到	yù dào	vc.	encounter; meet
59.	汇票	huìpiào	n.	money order
60.	非要	fēi yào		must; be determined (to do something)
61.	多事	duō shì	vo.	meddle
62.	既然	jìrán	conj.	since; now that
63.	姑奶奶	gūnǎinai	n.	grandaunt
64.	荒郊野外	huāngjiāo yěwài		wilderness
65.	这哪儿跟哪儿	zhè nǎr gēn nǎr		（see note 10）

吕　青：是我自己给的！我的**良心**让我这么做的。这样吧，我
　　　　们去**公安局**，到时候你可以说不认识我，就当是个**目
　　　　击证人**，如果有麻烦，我一个人**兜着**^{N11}，怎么样？

（画外音：既然看见了，我就觉得有这个责任……）

滕　超：**青青**！等等我——！

66.	良心	liángxīn	n.	conscience
67.	公安局	gōng'ānjú	n.	police station; public security bureau
68.	目击	mùjī	v.	witness
69.	证人	zhèng·rén	n.	witness
70.	兜（着）	dōu（zhe）	v.	(see note 11)
71.	青青	Qīngqīng	N.	(a nickname for Lü Qing)

注释 Notes

1. "有两下子":

意思是"有本领"，用于称赞人。口语。

"有两下子": This colloquialism is often used to praise someone for having the talent or abilities for a certain purpose.

（1）没想到你还有这两下子。

I didn't know you are actually so talented.

（2）他真有两下子，一下子就把小偷儿抓住了。

He was really something, and caught the thief in no time.

（3）A：你今天翻译当得不错嘛！

You did a good job in your translation today.

B：没有两下子，我敢答应给你们当翻译吗？

If I don't know one thing or two, would I have the guts to be your translator?

2. "此地不可久留":

"此"的意思是"这"，书面语，"可"的意思是"可以、应该"，"久留"的意思是"长时间停留"。这句话的意思是"不应该在这个地方停留很长时间（否则很危险，会有麻烦等）"。

"此地不可久留"："此" is a literary equivalent for the more colloquial "这", and "可" stands for "可以". "久留" means "to stay for long". The sentence thus means "One should not stay at this place for long (otherwise it could lead to trouble or danger)".

3. "那里好像还有别的什么吧":

这句话的意思是："那里还有别的（什么）东西吧？"

The question asks：There seems to be something else there, right?

4. "你怎么不想想后果":

这是一个反问句，意思是："你应该想想后果"。"后果"的意思是最后的结果，通常指不好的结果。

This rhetorical question actually suggests：You must think of the consequence. "后果" literally means "最后的结果" (final result, consequence), and it is usually in a negative sense.

(1) 他做事从来不想后果，吃了很多亏。

He never thought of the consequence of his actions, and had often to pay for it.

(2) 开车闯红灯的后果是很严重的。

The consequence of running through a red light is very serious.

(3) 你抄网上的论文，骗老师，想过后果吗？

You cheated your teacher by plagiarizing the thesis from the internet. Did you ever think of the consequence?

5. "多一事不如少一事"：

俗语。意思是"多管一件事，不如少管一件事"，说话人这样说时，是怕管别人的事会给自己带来麻烦。

"多一事不如少一事"：This popular saying literally means it is better to have one matter less than one more. It describes the mentality that one should avoid trouble whenever possible.

(1) 多一事不如少一事，你懂吗？你把它交给警察，也许警察能找到失主，可到时候咱们麻烦就大了！

Don't borrow trouble for yourself—do you understand? If you turn it in to the police, they will probably find the owner. But then it will be a big problem for us!

(2) A：你看那两个人在打架呢。

Look! Those two guys are fighting.

B：快走吧，别管他们，多一事不如少一事。

Hurry up. That's none of your business. Let's avoid trouble wherever possible.

6. "退一步说"：

在辩论问题时，"退一步说"引出一种假设，这个假设可能比实际或想象的情况好一点，程度低一点等等。

Literally, "退一步说" means "to take a step back and speak from that position". It is often used in a debate, where the speaker uses it to introduce a supposed situation which is somewhat better than that in reality. E. g.：

(1) 滕超：你也太天真了吧你！失主是谁？是个什么样的人？你知道吗？到时候失主愣说手袋里有一千块钱，有一万块钱，要是再说卡里有一百万，你怎么办？

Teng Chao：Aren't you being too naïve? Who is the owner? What kind of person is she? Do you have any idea? If she says there were a thousand dollars in the handbag，or even ten thousand，and if she also says there were one million dollars on the card，what will you do?

吕青：失主会吗？

Lü Qing：Would the owner say that?

滕超：好，咱再退一步说，就算失主不会，可这也是个刑事案件啊，到时候警察三天一调查，五天一取证，你就甭想消停了！

Teng Chao：OK，let's suppose she won't. Even so, this is a criminal case，and the police will come to question you today and ask you for evidence tomorrow. And you won't have your own life then!

（2）A：这个工作可能不是长期的，我不想做。

This is not a permanent job. I won't take it.

B：你怎么知道这个工作不是长期的？你现在没有工作，没有收入。退一步说，就算这个工作不是长期的，能解决你眼前的困难也好啊。

How do you know it's not a permanent job? You're now unemployed and have no income. OK，suppose it's indeed only a temporary job. Even so，it can at least relieve your current difficulties.

7. "三天……，五天……"：

表示"经常、很频繁"的意思。

This structure "三天……，五天……" denotes a high frequency as perceived by the speaker.

（1）到时候警察三天一调查，五天一取证，你就甭想消停了！

At that time the police will come to question you today and ask you for evidence tomorrow. You won't have your own life then!

（2）我们公司会特别多，三天一小会，五天一大会，把人烦死了。

We have so many meetings in our company，a small one today and a big one tomorrow. I'm bothered to death.

（3）三班的考试真多，三天一个小测验，五天一个大考，学生忙极了。

There are so many tests for Class Three，a quiz today and an exam to-morrow. The students are awfully busy.

8. "对于……来说"：

"对……来说"引出说话人对人或事物的判断或看法。如果所涉及的是人，那个人不一定有同样的看法。

This structure introduces the speaker's own judgment on something or a certain situation，which may or may not agree with the judgment of the party directly involved as indicated by the noun or pronoun following "对于".

(1) 那个合同和汇票对于他来说也许很重要呢？

That contract and the money order can be very important for him.

在这句话里，"对于……来说"引出说话人的看法，至于"对于"后边的"他"（所涉及的人），不一定认为"合同和汇票重要"。

In the above sentence，the structure "对于……来说" introduces the speaker's opinion，which is not necessarily the same as that of the person indicated by "他"，who is directly involved in the situation.

(2) 爸爸：对于你来说，现在最重要的是考上一个好的学校。

Father：For you，the most important thing is to get admitted to a good school.

儿子：我觉得上好学校太贵，将来不一定能找到好的工作。

Son：I think a good school is too expensive，and does not guarantee a good job in the future.

(3) 对我来说，钱不重要，快乐最重要。

For me，money is not important. The most important thing is happiness.

(4) 对于这个公司来说，现在最重要的是取得顾客的信任。

For this company，the most important thing now is to win the confidence of the customers.

9. "多事"：

意思是：做没有必要的、多余的事。

"多事" means "to do what is unnecessary" or "to bother about other people's business".

(1) 咱们还是别多这个事了。

Let's not poke our noses into that.

（2）你这个人真多事，小偷儿没有偷你的东西，你干吗管？他找人打你怎么办？

You're really meddlesome. The thief didn't steal anything from you, and why should you bother? What if he gets people to beat you?

（3）他真多事，别人穿什么衣服他都要管。

He is really meddling, and is even nosy about the way others dress.

10. "这哪儿跟哪儿啊"：

意思是：这两件事（或事情跟人）没有关系。口语。

This colloquial expression stresses the irrelevance between two things or between something and somebody.

（1）姑奶奶，荒郊野外的，哪儿来的责任啊？责任，这哪儿跟哪儿啊，谁给咱责任啦？

My good lady, we are in the middle of wilderness, and you speak about responsibility! What does this have to do with responsibility? And who's given us the responsibility?

（2）你说我要骗你的钱？这哪儿跟哪儿啊？我不过想帮你买便宜东西。

Did you say I wanted to swindle you out of your money? That's sheer nonsense! I was just trying to help you get some cheapies.

（3）你说那个单位请你去工作？这哪儿跟哪儿啊？他们不过是请你给他们的产品提提意见。

Did you say they wanted to hire you? How could that be the case? They were just asking for your opinions on their products.

11. "兜着"：

意思是：承担、负责任。口语。

The colloquial term "兜着" means to shoulder all responsibility and to answer for all possible consequences.

（1）如果有麻烦，我一个人兜着。

If there is any trouble, I'll take full responsibility for it.

（2）出了事，你兜着？

If it goes wrong, will you take it all upon yourself?

（3）这件事很麻烦，你别多事，出了问题，你吃不了，兜着走。

It's a troublesome matter and you should keep away from it. If something goes wrong, you will land yourself in serious trouble.

"吃不了兜着走"是一句俗语，意思也是"出了问题得承担一切后果”。

The popular saying "吃不了兜着走" literally means "to take all leftovers from the dining table in a bag". Metaphorically，if refers to a situation where one has to bear all the consequences of a bad action.

听说练习　Listening & Speaking Exercises

一、课文理解 Text Comprehension

（一）根据故事情节选择适当的答案

Please choose the most appropriate answer based on the story

1. 吕青和滕超在哪儿呢？（　　）
   A. 家具店　　　　　　B. 一个人很少的地方　　C. 学校

2. 吕青为什么喜欢欧式家具？（　　）
   A. 体现时尚　　　　B. 非常浪漫　　　　　C. 可以听到小夜曲

3. 他们走路时突然发现了一个（　　）
   A. 大款　　　　　　B. 手包　　　　　　　C. 手机

4. 滕超认为他们应该马上离开这儿，因为他（　　）
   A. 怕警察　　　　　B. 怕麻烦　　　　　　C. 怕小偷儿

5. 吕青想到的只是失主的（　　）
   A. 汇款收据　　　　B. 麻烦　　　　　　　C. 合同

6. 最后滕超跟吕青一起去了公安局，是因为他觉得（　　）
   A. 这也是他的责任　　B. 吕青需要帮助　　　C. 他要当目击证人

（二）根据课文判断下面句子意思的正误

State whether the following statements are true or false based on the story

1. （　　）吕青认为在一个布满欧式家具的房间里听小夜曲会更浪漫。

2. （　　）滕超和吕青散步的时候发现了一个大款淘汰的手包。

3. （　　）手包里有钱、手机等值钱的东西。

4. （　　）吕青认为他们发现手包的地方是大款的手包被偷的地方。

5. （　　）小偷把包里的二十万元钱都拿走了。

6. （　　）吕青怕警察认为是他们拿走了包里的东西，所以想赶快走开。

7.（　　）滕超认为多一事不如少一事，要是他们把这个包送到公安局，会给他们带来很多麻烦。

8.（　　）吕青认为虽然此事可能会给他们带来麻烦，但是失主的麻烦更大。

（三）先听故事叙述，然后复述故事
Listen to the narrative first and then retell the story

　　吕青和滕超在河边散步时发现了一个手包。开始他们以为是哪个大款扔了的，后来发现里面有一张二十万元的电汇收据，还有一张名片，但是一分钱也没有。

　　滕超认为一定是小偷在别的地方偷了这个包，拿走了手包里的钱、手机等值钱的东西，然后将手包扔到这个偏僻的地方。吕青要找失主，可是滕超认为多一事不如少一事。他说如果把它交给警察，也许警察能找到失主，可是也可能会怀疑是他们拿了值钱的东西，失主也可能会说手袋里有很多钱。就算这些事不发生，警察经常找你取证，也很麻烦。

　　吕青不同意滕超的看法，认为那个合同和汇票对失主一定很重要，他可能遇到的麻烦更大。如果他们没有看到这个包，那和他们没有关系；但是既然看到了，她觉得就有责任找到失主。吕青坚持要把包送到公安局去。滕超最后也觉得自己有责任，就和吕青一起去公安局了。

■ 二、词语使用 Application of Vocabulary and Grammar

（一）选择题
Choose the item that is grammatically correct

1. 滕超，你怎么就单单没有考虑＿＿＿＿＿那个手袋的失主会遇到什么麻烦呢？

　　A. 好　　　　　　　　B. 到　　　　　　　　C. 清楚

2. 你说这手包肯定有问题？你＿＿＿＿＿吓唬我啊。

　　A. 特别　　　　　　　B. 可别　　　　　　　C. 肯定

3. 你把它交给警察，也许警察能找到失主，可到时候咱们麻烦＿＿＿＿＿大了！

　　A. 会　　　　　　　　B. 就　　　　　　　　C. 很

4. 小偷偷了这个包，拿走了里边儿值钱的东西，＿＿＿＿＿找个偏僻的地方将手包扔了。

    A. 后来   B. 以后   C. 然后

5. 那个合同和汇票＿＿＿＿＿＿他来说也许很重要，失主的麻烦会比我们的大得多。

    A. 对于   B. 关于   C. 看来

6. 姑奶奶，荒郊野外的，＿＿＿＿＿＿来的责任啊？

    A. 哪ル   B. 谁   C. 怎么

（二）选择题

Circle the answer that best reflects the meaning of the underlined portion of the sentence

1. 咱们玩ル得好好的，你干嘛<u>非</u>要多这个事ル啊？（   ）

    A. 是非

    B. 非常

    C. 一定

    D. 肯定

2. 可这也是个刑事案件啊，到时候警察三天一调查，五天一取证，你就甭想<u>消停</u>了！（   ）

    A. 安静

    B. 休息

    C. 平静

    D. 安全

3. 你也太天真了吧你！到时候失主<u>愣</u>说手袋里有一万块钱，你怎么办？（   ）

    A. 生气

    B. 坚持

    C. 一再

    D. 肯定

4. 你说你没看见，人家会信吗？人家就不会相信咱们<u>把钱给昧了</u>？

                                         （   ）

    A. 把钱丢了

    B. 把钱藏起来了

    C. 把钱给妹妹了

D. 把钱给扔了

5. 多一事不如少一事（　　）
   A. 多一事比少一事好
   B. 少一事比多一事好
   C. 少事好
   D. 多事好

6. 这是哪个大款啊，这么好的一个手包就淘汰了？（　　）
   A. 洗了
   B. 旧了
   C. 扔了
   D. 坏了

7. 有道理！行啊，没想到你还有这两下子，福尔摩斯先生。（　　）
   A. 知道的事情还真不少
   B. 偷过东西
   C. 去过两次
   D. 做过警察

（三）选择适当的词语，替换句中的画线部分
Choose the most appropriate words to replace the underlined parts

> A. 此地不可久留　　B. 多事　　　　C. 兜着　　　D. 退一步说
> E. 有两下子　　　　F. 这哪儿跟哪儿啊　　G. 多一事不如少一事
> H. 三天……，五天……

1. 能不管的事就不管，免得给你带来麻烦。
2. 这手包肯定有问题。咱们最好赶快离开这儿！
3. 没想到他还真有本事，一下子就把小偷儿抓住了。
4. 中文课的考试真多，今天笔试，明天口试，学生忙极了。
5. 你说失主和警察不会不相信我们，好，咱就往好的地方想，就算失主和警察相信我们，可是到时候警察三天一调查，五天一取证，你就甭想消停了。
6. 你真爱管闲事，小偷儿没有偷你的东西，你干吗管？他找人打你怎么办？
7. 这件事很麻烦，你别多事，出了问题，你一个人负责？
8. 你说那个单位请你去工作？这跟工作没关系。他们不过是请你给他们

的产品提提意见。

（四）角色扮演 Role play

Make a dialogue with a classmate. One party plays Teng Chao, and the other plays Lü Qing. Your dialogue should incorporate the provided items.

滕超	吕青
Upon discovering a very nice handbag, your first thought is that it must have been discarded by a rich man. After seeing what is inside, however, you are convinced that it is a criminal case. Fearing the endless trouble that would result if you reported the incident to the police, you strongly suggest to your girlfriend that the two of you walk away from it at once.	Urged by your boyfriend to walk away from the handbag, you are troubled by the possible anxiety and trouble the owner of the handbag might suffer. Your conscience makes you believe that it is a person's responsibility to do the right thing even though your involvement would interrupt one's otherwise peaceful life and could also bring you a lot of trouble.

滕超		吕青	
1. 大款	2. 淘汰	1. 吓唬	2. 有两下子
3. 肯定	4. 说明	3. 电汇收据	4. 名片
5. 值钱的东西	6. 偏僻	5. 根本	6. 确实
7. 此地不可久留	8. 后果	7. 单单	8. 考虑
9. 多一事不如少一事……		9. 对于	10. 重要
10. 给昧了	11. 天真	11. 既然……就……	
12. 退一步说		12. 责任	13. 良心
13. 三天……，五天……		14. 公安局	15. 目击证人
14. 甭想……	15. 干吗非……	16. 兜着	

■ 三、课堂讨论 Discussion

1. 你对滕超的"多一事不如少一事"有什么看法？

2. 要是你是滕超或吕青，你会怎么做？

3. 滕超是坏人吗？像滕超这样的人多不多？为什么？

4. 你对吕青说的"如果我们没有看到，那和我们没有关系；但是既然看到了，我就觉得我们有这个责任……"有什么看法？

5. 为什么最后滕超要吕青等等他？

第十课 合适不合适

Appropriate or Not

编剧：王源源

人物 (Characters)

娜娜 （Nàna）——女青年。

娜娜老公 （Nàna lǎogōng）

邻居若干 （Línjū ruògān）

课　文　Text

娜　娜：嗯，你看咱家**憨憨**洗完澡，多漂亮多**精神**哪！是不是，憨
　　　　憨他爸？

娜娜老公：行了行了[N1]，别瞎叫了！谁是它爸爸呀！

娜　娜：你瞧啊，爸爸对妈妈多**凶**啊！是不是，憨憨？哎呀……来，
　　　　过来，爸爸坏，对不对？哎，憨憨，妈妈给憨憨**吹个风**，
　　　　好不好？

---

1. 老公	lǎogōng	n.	husband (colloquial term)
2. 憨憨	Hānhān	N.	(name of a dog)
3. 精神	jīngshen	adj.	lively; vigorous
4. 凶	xiōng	adj.	vicious; fierce; mean
5. 吹（个）风	chuī (ge) fēng	vo.	blow (hair)

娜娜老公：哎，我说，你可别**动**我那个新的啊，为了你这宝贝憨憨，我已经**妥协**买个新的啦！哎，你还想让我怎么着？老婆，这小狗不会也**喜新厌旧**^{N2}吧。

娜　　娜：**小气鬼**，好好好，爸爸生气了！那咱不用那个，咱用旧的啊。爸爸真是的^{N3}，那么大岁数，还跟咱们憨憨**抢**。

娜娜老公：老婆，我**求**求你了行不行啊？它不就是条狗嘛，你至于吗^{N4}？哎，你不怕邻居们笑话呀？

娜　　娜：谁呀？谁笑话？他敢！看看咱们憨憨多可爱呀，多漂亮呀！谁都会喜欢的！才^{N5}不像你那么没**爱心**呢！是不是？再说了，**当初**还是你抱回来它的呢！现在你**嫌弃**它呀？

娜娜老公：我当初抱它回来不是为了怕你**寂寞**、让你开心嘛！再说了，我也没嫌弃它呀。我就是觉得呀，您这种**叫法**有点儿**夸张**了。

娜　　娜：对呀，现在我是开心啦，那你还说什么呀！

娜娜老公：行行行^{N6}，我**说不过**你，行吗？说不过你，你爱怎么着怎么着吧^{N7}。

6.	动	dòng	v.	touch
7.	妥协	tuǒxié	v.	compromise
8.	喜新厌旧	xǐ xīn yàn jiù		(see note 2)
9.	小气鬼	xiǎoqìguǐ	n.	mean person (as used in this story); miser
10.	抢	qiǎng	v.	fight (with someone over something, as used in this story)
11.	求	qiú	v.	beg
12.	爱心	àixīn	n.	love; compassion
13.	当初	dāngchū	t.	in the beginning; at first
14.	嫌弃	xiánqì	v.	dislike and avoid; disfavor
15.	寂寞	jìmò	adj.	lonely; lonesome
16.	叫法	jiàofǎ	n.	the way one addresses someone
17.	夸张	kuāzhāng	adj.	exaggerated
18.	说不过	shuō bu guò	vc.	not as eloquent as...

娜　　娜：去育新小区。

娜　　娜：哎，您等会儿，先把那窗户摇上一下，我们憨憨生病了。

出租车司机：好。

娜　　娜：师傅待会儿您开车时候得慢点儿开，我们憨憨晕车。

出租车司机：啊，好！

娜　　娜：来，咱憨憨出来透透气啦……

出租车司机：哟，小姐，原来您这是条狗啊！

娜　　娜：什么狗啊，咱叫憨憨！来，叫叔叔好！

出租车司机：看来您是把狗当儿子养啦！

娜　　娜：咳，您还说错了，咱们是小姑娘，是女儿！

娜　　娜：憨憨你慢点儿慢点儿！妈妈追不上你了！

小　姑　娘：阿姨，您怎么能让您的狗随地大小便呢？

19. 育新小区	Yùxīn Xiǎoqū	N.	Yuxin Subdivision
20. 窗户	chuānghu	n.	window
21. 摇上	yáo shàng	vc.	roll (a window) up (to close the window of a car)
22. 待会儿	dāi huìr		wait for a minute
23. 晕车	yùn chē	vo.	carsick
24. 透气	tòu qì	vo.	get fresh air
25. 原来	yuánlái	adv./adj.	(it) turns out
26. 叔叔	shūshu	n.	(child's form of address for any young man of one generation its senior) uncle; father's younger brother
27. 姑娘	gūniang	n.	girl; daughter
28. 追不上	zhuī bu shàng	vc.	cannot catch up (with someone)
29. 随地大小便	suídì dàxiǎobiàn		relieve (oneself) anywhere

娜　娜：哟，憨憨，你看小姐姐都生气了。**咱家**憨憨哪，**平时**可[N8]乖了，就是这两天有点**闹肚子**，对不对？

小姑娘：那您可以从后边把它**捡**起来呀！这样就不会影响别人了！我以前就**踩**过一次，**恶心**死了！

娜　娜：哟，那你以后可得**小心**点ﾉ了！憨憨，来，咱跟小姐姐再见！来……Bye bye，再见，走了。

小姑娘：谁是它小姐姐？我才不做狗的姐姐呢！要做你自己做去吧[N9]，哼！

娜　娜：来，跟叔叔打个招呼。

娜　娜：叫阿姨好，叫阿姨好。哎，程哥，叫**程大大**好，哎，你看，我们**配**(的) 衣服好看吗？……前两天生病了吃药打针一声都没**吭**……我给它买了件衣服，好看吧？

程××：我还有事……

30. 咱家	zán jiā		my (as used in this story)
31. 平时	píngshí	t.	ordinarily; normally
32. 闹肚子	nào dùzi	vo.	have diarrhea
33. 捡	jiǎn	v.	pick up
34. 踩	cǎi	v.	step upon; stamp
35. 恶心	ěxin	adj./v.	disgusting
36. 小心	xiǎoxīn	v./adj.	be careful; be cautious
37. 程	Chéng	N.	family name
38. 大大	dàda	n.	(child's form of address for any man elder than his/her father) uncle; father's older brother (mostly used in the Northern dialect)
39. 配	pèi	v.	match (color, style, etc.)
40. 吭	kēng	v.	utter a sound or a word

娜　娜：来，跟程大大再见，再见，走喽！

小姑娘：娜娜快走啊，娜娜快走啊！走啊！娜娜快走啊，走啊！快
　　　　走啊！走啊！

娜　娜：你叫谁呢？

小姑娘：我叫它呢！

娜　娜：**闹了半天**[N10] 你叫狗呢？

小姑娘：对呀。

娜　娜：你怎么让狗叫我的名字呀？

小姑娘：阿姨，您也叫娜娜呀？

娜　娜：什么呀！我就是叫娜娜。我是人，它是狗，我叫了它就不
　　　　能叫！再说了，你这狗长这么**寒碜**，它怎么能叫"娜
　　　　娜"呢？

小姑娘：我从小就叫它娜娜。

41. 喽	lou	interj.	a sentence particle，same as 了 here
42. 闹了半天	nào le bàn tiān		（see note 10）
43. 寒碜	hánchen	adj.	ugly

娜　娜：**岂有此理**！你不许叫啦！

老奶奶：哟，你好好地说，我们的狗一下**吓着**你啦？

娜　娜：**吓倒是**没吓着^{N11}，可是你这孩子太不**懂事**，让狗叫我的名字！您是她家长吧？您也不管管她！

老奶奶：哎呀，姑娘呀，我们家的狗就叫娜娜！真是**碰巧**了，真是对不起您！**街坊**邻居们讲呀，您有的时候也把别人叫成狗的**爷爷**、叔叔、姐姐**什么的**^{N12}，这好像就不太合适了吧！喜欢**宠物自然**没什么，但是如果人狗不分**乱叫一气**^{N13}，那就不合适了，你说是吧，孩子？

44. 岂有此理	qǐ yǒu cǐ lǐ		ridiculous; nonsense
45. 老奶奶	lǎonǎinai	n.	grandmother; granny
46. 吓着	xià zhao	vc.	frighten
47. 倒是	dàoshì	adv.	but instead; used to express what is contrary to facts
48. 懂事	dǒng shì	vo.	be sensible; intelligent
49. 碰巧	pèngqiǎo	adj.	coincident
50. 街坊	jiēfang	n.	neighbor
51. 爷爷	yéye	n.	(paternal) grandfather; grandpa
52. 什么的	shénme de		... etc.
53. 宠物	chǒngwù	n.	pet; pet animal
54. 自然	zìrán	adv./adj.	normally; certainly
55. 乱	luàn	adj.	indiscriminately (as used in this context)
56. 一气	yí qì		(see note 13)

注释　Notes

1. **"行了行了"**:

　　见第八课注释 6。Refer to note 6 of Lesson 8.

2. **"喜新厌旧"**:

　　意思是：喜欢新的，讨厌抛弃旧的。原来主要指男女感情方面用情不专。本剧的意思是"喜欢新电吹风，讨厌旧电吹风"。

　　"喜新厌旧" means "to like the new and forget the old". It usually refers to a sexual relationship. In the text，Nana's husband wants to say "I don't think a small dog could abandon old things for new things just like humans can be fickle with affection."

（1）这小狗不会也喜新厌旧吧？

　　I hope you will not say this small dog is also "fond of the new and tired of the old."

（2）他这个人喜新厌旧，经常换女朋友。

　　He is a fickle lover，and changes girlfriends often.

（3）你跟女朋友不好了，不是喜新厌旧吧？

　　You're not on good terms with your girlfriend. You're not cheating on her（with a new girl），are you?

3. **"真是的"**:

　　用来表达不满意的情绪。口语。

　　"真是的" is a colloquial term that is used to express dissatisfaction or complaint.

（1）爸爸真是的，那么大岁数，还跟咱们憨憨抢。

　　Come on Baba，how could you，at your age，possibly fight with our Hanhan.

（2）你真是的，这么一点儿作业都没做完，太懒了。

　　You didn't even finish this small amount of homework! You really are too lazy!

（3）这个人真是的，老跟别人借钱。

This person—seriously! Always borrowing money from people!

4. **"至于吗"**:

参见第二课注释19。Refer to note 19 of Lesson 8.

5. **"才"**:

"才"可以加强语气，多用在否定句中。口语。

"才", very colloquial, is used to emphasize the tone. It often occurs in a negative sentence.

(1) 看看咱们憨憨，多可爱呀，多漂亮呀！谁都会喜欢的！才不像你那么没良心呢。

Look at our Hanhan, how cute he is! How pretty! Everyone loves him. He's not like you, who doesn't have a kind heart at all.

(2) A：大家都去参加小李的生日晚会了，你也去吧。

Everyone has gone to Xiao Li's birthday party. You should also go.

B：我才不去呢，我的生日晚会他也没来。

Why should I go, since he didn't come to my birthday party?

(3) 买房子？我才不买呢，没钱。

Me, buy a house? I don't have the money.

6. **"行行行"**:

"行"有"可以"的意思。连说三个"行"，有时表示"非常同意"。娜娜的老公说："行行行，我说不过你，行吗？"表达了一种"没有办法，无可奈何"的心情。

"行" means "OK". When said repeatedly, it indicates the speaker's agreement. However, it can also reflects the speaker's helplessness or impatience. For example, when Nana's husband says "Ok, ok, ok, I can't argue over you, alright?", it shows his helplessness in the situation and readiness to give in.

7. **"你爱怎么着怎么着吧"**:

意思是：如果你想怎么样，你就怎么样吧，我管不了（不管）你。口语。

娜娜老公说："行行行，我说不过你，行吗？说不过你，你爱怎么着怎么着吧。"表示虽然他不同意娜娜的做法，但是管不了娜娜，对娜娜没有办法。

"你爱怎么着怎么着吧", a colloquial expression, meaning "do as you like". Often, the speaker uses this expression to indicate that he is giving in to an argument.

8. "可" (二)：

"可" 在感叹句中可以表示程度高并加强语气。口语。

"可"，colloquial，is used to intensify the tone that suggests a greater degree of a state.

(1) 憨憨平时可乖了。

Hanhan is usually well behaved.

(2) 今天我可累了，不能做功课。

I can't do any study today. I'm really tired.

(3) 她男朋友对他可好了，所以他一走，她可想他了。

Her boyfriend is very nice to her, and she misses him terribly every time he is away.

9. "要做你自己做去吧"：

这个句子的意思是：如果要做，你就自己做去吧。汉语口语中的句子经常不用关联词语。见第六课注释9。

"要做你自己做去吧"，(If) you want to do it,（then）do it yourself. The conjunctions, i. e., "要是" and "就" are omitted, as it often occurs in colloqial speech. Also refer to note 9 of Lesson 6.

10. "闹了半天"：

"半天" 表示时间很长。"闹" 可以表示 "做、弄" 的意思。当发生找人找了很久才找到，或听别人说话听了很久才明白等情况时，可以先说 "闹了半天"。

"半天" refers to "a very long time". "闹" means "to do, or handle". "闹了半天" means "after all that", "it turns out". This expression is used when the speaker, after spending much time, eventually found something, or realized something.

(1) 闹了半天你叫狗呢?

After all that, it turns out you're calling your dog.

(2) 闹了半天你在这儿呢，我找了你好长时间了。

I've been looking for you for a long time, and it turns out you've been here all along.

(3) 闹了半天你们认识啊? 我还想把他介绍给你呢。

It turns out you two know each other. I was just about to introduce him to you.

11. **"吓倒是没吓着……"：**

"倒是"这里表示实际情况和事实或所想的相反，后边常跟着"可是/但是……"。口语。

"倒是" is usually used in colloquial speech. It suggests that the situation is just the opposite of what is expected. This expression is commonly followed by "but/however".

(1) 老奶奶：您好！是不是我家狗吓着你了？

娜　娜：吓倒是没吓着，可是你这孩子太不懂事，让狗叫我的名字！

Nana: Oh, no, it's not that the dog scared me. However, your child is very bad-mannered, naming the dog with my name.

(2) A：你没找到工作吗？怎么这么不高兴？

How come you are so unhappy? Did you not find a job?

B：工作倒是找到了，只是不太好。

I did find a job, but it's not really satisfactory.

(3) A：今天你怎么这么早就回来了？没上课吗？

Why are you back so early today? Did you not go to class?

B：课倒是上了，可是我不舒服，所以没下课就回来了。

I did go to class, but I didn't feel well, so I came back before the class was over.

12. **"……什么的"：**

用在一个词或几个并列的词（或短语）后，表示"等等"的意思。口语。

"……什么的" a colloquial term, has a similar function as "……etc".

(1) 街坊邻居们讲呀，您有的时候也把别人叫成狗的爷爷、叔叔、姐姐什么的，这，好像就不太合适了吧！

All the neighbors say that you sometimes address people as your dog's grandpa, uncle, sister, etc. Is this proper?

(2) 我刚才上街买了水果、面包什么的。

I just bought some fruit, bread, etc.

(3) 他不喜欢看书，只喜欢唱歌、跳舞什么的。

He doesn't like to read. He only enjoys singing and dancing, etc.

13. **"（乱叫）一气"：**

"气"有动量词"阵"的意思，常含有贬义。口语。

"气" is a measure word for an action in colloquial speech. It has the similar meaning of "阵" ("a while"). It often has derogative connotation.

(1) 喜欢宠物自然没什么，但是如果人狗不分乱叫一气，那就不合适了吧！

It is nothing wrong to love pets，but it is improper if（you）mix pets with humans.

(2) 孩子们在教室里胡闹一气，把教室搞得乱七八糟。

The kids fooled around in the classroom，and made a huge mess there.

再如"（打电话）乱打一气""瞎唱一气""胡说一气"等。

"一气" also occurs in these phrases such as "make useless calls"，"sing nonsense"，"speak nonsense" etc.

有些方言用"一气"是不含贬义的，如：

In some dialects，"一气" does not have negative sense，for example：

(3) 她哭了一气不哭了。

She cried for a while and then stopped.

听说练习　Listening & Speaking Exercises

■ 一、课文理解 Text Comprehension

（一）根据故事情节选择适当的答案

Please choose the most appropriate answer based on the story

1. 娜娜的老公不高兴是因为（　　）

　　A. 娜娜给狗用他的新电吹风

　　B. 娜娜给狗洗澡了

　　C. 娜娜把他叫成狗的爸爸

2. 娜娜的老公觉得娜娜（　　）

　　A. 只爱狗，不爱他　　　　B. 喜新厌旧　　　　C. 人狗不分

3. 憨憨是（　　）

　　A. 娜娜的老公抱回来的

　　B. 娜娜买来的

　　C. 朋友送来的

4. 小姑娘告诉娜娜不应该让她的狗（　　）

　　A. 闹肚子　　　　　　　　B. 随地大小便　　　　C. 叫她姐姐

5. 娜娜认为（　　）

　　A. 小姑娘自己走路应该小心

　　B. 憨憨影响了别人

　　C. 憨憨今天闹肚子

6. 娜娜生小姑娘的气，是因为（　　）

　　A. 小姑娘的狗长得不好看

　　B. 小姑娘不喜欢她的狗

　　C. 小姑娘的狗跟娜娜叫一样的名字

7. 老奶奶觉得娜娜不应该（　　）

　　A. 那么爱狗

B. 把她的邻居都叫做狗爷爷、奶奶、姐姐什么的

C. 不许小姑娘的狗叫"娜娜"

（二）**根据课文判断下面句子意思的正误**

State whether the following statements are true or false based on the story

1.（　　）娜娜的老公不愿意跟憨憨用一个电吹风。

2.（　　）娜娜的老公觉得娜娜对狗像对人一样。

3.（　　）娜娜的老公现在不喜欢狗了。

4.（　　）出租车司机开始的时候以为憨憨是一个小孩子。

5.（　　）小姑娘不喜欢娜娜因为她让憨憨随地大小便。

6.（　　）娜娜不喜欢小姑娘因为小姑娘的狗长得很难看。

7.（　　）小姑娘以前不知道她的狗跟娜娜叫一样的名字。

8.（　　）老奶奶觉得娜娜把邻居叫成狗的爷爷、奶奶、姐姐是对人不尊重（不合适）。

（三）**先听故事叙述，然后复述故事**

Listen to the narrative first and then retell the story

　　娜娜很喜欢宠物，娜娜的老公给她抱回来一只小狗，他们叫它憨憨。娜娜每天不但给憨憨很多好吃的东西，而且还给它穿衣服。最近，娜娜把老公叫成狗的爸爸，把邻居叫成狗的爷爷、奶奶、姐姐什么的，这让大家很不舒服。

　　今天娜娜带憨憨出去走路的时候发生了几件不高兴的事：憨憨随地大小便的时候，一个小姑娘告诉娜娜应该捡起来，要不然会影响别人；后来，娜娜又发现小姑娘的狗跟她的名字一样；还有，邻居老奶奶说娜娜不应该人狗不分。娜娜回家以后一直在想她哪儿做得不合适。

■ 二、词语使用 Application of Vocabulary and Grammar

（一）**选择题**

Choose the item that is grammatically correct

1. 我弟弟也_____，我爸爸刚给他买的新手机，用了一个星期就丢了。这已经是第三个了。

　　A. 真夸张　　　B. 真是的　　　C. 真喜新厌旧　　D. 岂有此理

2. 司机师傅，麻烦您把窗户摇_____一点，透透气。这车里面空气不太好。

　　A. 下来　　　　B. 过去　　　　C. 起来　　　　D. 上去

3. 我的同屋昨天晚上出去到今天早上还没回来。我紧张死了，给认识她的人都打了电话，到处找她。_____，她在图书馆待了一个晚上，写学期报告来着。

A. 真是的　　　　　　　B. 闹了半天

C. 再说了　　　　　　　D. 岂有此理

4. A：昨天我去看病的时候，我的医生告诉我不能再胖了。

B：那你得少吃肉，少吃糖了。像你现在这样_____哪能不胖呢？

A. 乱喝一气　　　　　　B. 乱做一气

C. 乱吃一气　　　　　　D. 乱说一气

5. A：我朋友的狗死了，她心疼（难过）得好几天没有吃饭了，连上班都快不能上了。

B：_____，不就是一条狗吗！

A. 真夸张　　　　　　　B. 岂有此理

C. 至于吗　　　　　　　D. 行了行了

（二）选择题

Circle the answer that best reflects the meaning of the sentence

1. 小狗不会也喜新厌旧吧？（　　）

A. 小狗也喜欢新的东西不喜欢旧的东西。

B. 难道小狗也喜欢新的东西不喜欢旧的东西吗？

C. 小狗不会喜欢新的东西不喜欢旧的东西。

D. 小狗跟人一样。

2. 他也真是的，大学毕业一年了，还不找工作。（　　）

A. 他大学毕业一年了，可是还没有工作，这是真的。

B. 他大学毕业一年了，还不找工作，真不应该。

C. 他大学毕业一年以后才开始找工作。

D. 他大学毕业一年了，可是还没有找到工作。

3. 你家的狗吓倒是没吓着我，可是你的孩子太不懂事了。（　　）

A. 行了，行了，你家的狗没有吓着我，可是你家的孩子太不聪明。

B. 你家的狗不错，可是我不喜欢你的孩子。

C. 你家的狗并没有吓着我，可是你的孩子吓着我了。

D. 其实，你家的狗并没有吓着我，可是你的孩子对人太不客气了。

4. （我以为你在跟孩子说话呢），闹了半天，是条小狗啊！（　　）

A. 原来，你是在跟一条小狗说话呢！

B. 我听了半天的时间，才知道这是一条小狗。

C. 你的狗叫了半天时间，我才知道这是一条小狗。

D. 原来，你是在跟一条小狗闹呢！

5. 喜欢宠物自然没什么，但是如果人狗不分就不合适了。（　　）

A. 我们应该喜欢宠物，狗和人有很多一样的地方。

B. 喜欢宠物的人很多，可是把狗当做人的人不多。

C. 喜欢宠物当然可以，不过把狗当做人就不应该了。

D. 喜欢宠物没意思，把狗当做人就更没有意思了。

6. 什么？你给狗开生日晚会?! 我才没你那么爱狗呢！（　　）

A. 你给狗开生日晚会吗？我没有狗。

B. 你给狗开生日晚会吗？我不爱狗。

C. 难道你给狗开生日晚会吗？我可没有像你那样爱狗。

D. 你给狗开生日晚会吗？你太爱狗了！

7. 谁爱怎么着怎么着，我才不怕邻居笑话呢！（　　）

A. 我不怕笑话人的人。

B. 谁笑什么，我不在乎。

C. 谁笑话我？我真的不担心。

D. 谁喜欢怎么样，没关系，我一点儿都不在乎邻居笑话！

（三）选择适当的词语，替换句中的画线部分

Choose the most appropriate words to replace the underlined parts

A. 真是的	B. 才不……呢	C. 可 adj. 了	D. adj. 倒是不 adj.
E. 摇上	F. 把 X 当 Y 养	G. 行了行了	H. 要 V 你 V 吧

1. 我<u>真不应该</u>，怎么忘了在中国给我妈妈买件中国礼物了！

2. 昨天的考试<u>其实不难</u>，就是太长了。

3. 我今天还有很多作业要做呢，我<u>可不去看电影</u>！

4. 太冷了，司机师傅，能不能把窗户<u>关上</u>。

5. 娜娜对狗太好了，我看，她真是<u>养狗跟养孩子一样</u>。

6. 我现在闹肚子，不能喝啤酒，<u>如果你想喝，你就自己喝吧</u>。

7. 那个美国朋友中文说得<u>真好</u>，上次他给我打电话，我真以为是个中国人呢！

8. <u>好了好了</u>，别生气了，下次我一定不会忘了给你打电话。

（四）用所给词语完成对话

Complete the following dialogues with the items provided in the parenthesis

1. （行行行，要 V 你 V 吧）

    A：你想好了吗？点什么菜？

    B：来个排骨，怎么样？

    A：这个菜对身体不好，＿＿＿＿＿＿，反正我不吃。

    B：＿＿＿＿＿＿，不点这个菜了！

2. （至于吗，才不）

    A：上星期五考试没有考好，现在我想起来还觉得不高兴。

    B：＿＿＿＿＿＿，不就是一次考试吗？下次考好一点儿就行了！我
    ＿＿＿＿＿＿像你呢，为了一次考试，好几天都不高兴。

3. （乱叫一气，什么的，恶心死了）

    A：你认识娜娜吗？

    B：是不是那个每天都把别人叫成狗的哥哥、姐姐、弟弟＿＿＿＿＿＿
    那个人？

    A：对，我真不喜欢她这样＿＿＿＿＿＿。

    B：听了让人＿＿＿＿＿＿。

4. （adj. 倒是不/没 adj.，闹了半天）

    A：你去哪儿了？我在这儿等了半个小时了！

    B：我去宿舍找你去了，＿＿＿＿＿＿你在这儿等我呢！真对不起，电影
    晚了吧？

    A：＿＿＿＿＿＿，还有半个小时呢。

    B：我们走吧，我的车在路对面呢！

（五）角色扮演 Role play

Make a dialogue with a classmate. One party plays Nana, and the other plays Nana's husband. Your dialogue should incorporate the provided items.

娜娜的老公	娜娜
When you see your wife using your hair dryer to dry the dog, you are very upset. How can she treat the dog like a person? People are already laughing at her.	You can not see why he is so upset with this. Who cares what other people talk about? You just love your dog!

1. 刚买的	1. 行行行
2. 可别	2. 真是的
3. 不就是……	3. 谁爱 V 就 V
4. 笑话	4. 才不怕……

三、课堂讨论 Discussion

1. 娜娜的邻居对娜娜有什么看法？

2. 你对娜娜把狗当做孩子养有什么看法？

3. 在你看来，娜娜是一个什么样的人？

4. 从这个故事看，一般的中国人对狗的看法跟你们国家的人一样吗？

附录一：生词索引　Vocabulary Index

A

表现	biǎoxiàn	v./n.	behavior; conduct	7
憋死	biē sǐ	vc.	be suffocated to death	5
别价	biéjie	adv.	(see note 16)	2
博拉姆斯	Bólāmǔsī	N.	Johannes Brahms (19th-century German composer)	9
补	bǔ	v.	nourish body; make up for	2
不成	bùchéng	part.	(It is used to attach to the end of a sentence to indicate inference or a rhetorical question)	2
不及格	bù jígé		fail (an exam); flunk	5
不仅	bùjǐn	adv.	not only	5
不客气	bú kèqì		you are welcome	1
不如	bùrú	v.	not as good as	9
不要紧	bù yàojǐn		It doesn't matter	3
布满	bùmǎn	vc.	be covered by	9
布置	bùzhì	v.	assign (homework, etc.)	5
部门	bùmén	n.	department; branch; section; division	7

C

才智	cáizhì	n.	talent; gift	7
踩	cǎi	v.	step upon; stamp	10
采访	cǎifǎng	v.	interview	2
彩虹	cǎihóng	n.	rainbow	5
测试	cèshì	v.	test; assessment	7
噌噌见长	cēngcēng jiànzhǎng		(see note 7)	6
差点儿	chà diǎnr		almost	2
尝	cháng	v.	taste; try the flavor of	1
长城	Chángchéng	N.	Great Wall	1
长命百岁	cháng mìng bǎi suì		live to be hundred years old	1
长寿	chángshòu	adj.	long life; longevity	1
场合	chǎnghé	n.	site; venue; occasion	7
场所	chǎngsuǒ	n.	place; location; venue	7
抄	chāo	v.	copy; plagiarize; plagiary	5
朝阳门	Cháoyángmén	N.	(a place in Beijing)	7
程	Chéng	N.	family name	10
成功	chénggōng	v./n.	succeed; success	7
成绩	chéngjì	n.	grade; mark; achievement	5

乘客	chéngkè	n.	passenger	7
承认	chéngrèn	v.	admit（a mistake）	4
成心	chéngxīn	adv.	intentionally；deliberately	7
吃亏	chī kuī	vo.	suffer losses	8
冲	chōng	v.	dash；stride	3
宠物	chǒngwù	n.	pet；pet animal	10
抽屉	chōuti	n.	drawer	4
出租车	chūzūchē	n.	taxi	1
处	chù	n.	place；location	5
处长	chùzhǎng	n.	head of a department or office；section chief	3
窗户	chuānghu	n.	window	10
吹（个）风	chuī（ge）fēng	vo.	blow（hair）	10
纯情	chúnqíng	n.	pure feeling；innocent love	5
此地	cǐ dì		this place；here	9
聪明	cōngmíng	adj./n.	intelligent，wise；intelligence，wisdom	7
撮一顿	cuō yi dùn	vo.	have a good meal	6
错怪	cuòguài	v.	wrong（someone）	4
错误	cuòwù	n.	mistake；error	4

D

打饱嗝	dǎ bǎogé	vo.	belch	6
打开	dǎ kāi	vc.	open	7
打水漂	dǎ shuǐpiāo	vo.	（see note 9）	2
大大	dàda	n.	（child's form of address for any man elder than his/her father）uncle；father's older brother（mostly used in the Northern dialect）	10
大款	dàkuǎn	n.	person of wealth（colloq.）	9
大人	dàren	n.	adult；grown up	4
大声	dà shēng		loudly；in loud voice	7
大爷	dàye	n.	uncle（a respectful form of address for an elderly man）；father's elder brother	2
代表	dàibiǎo	v.	represent；be on behalf of	3
待会儿	dāi huìr		stay for a moment；wait a moment	3
待会儿	dāi huìr		wait for a minute	10
待会儿见	dāi huìr jiàn		see you later	6

待人接物	dài rén jiē wù		codes of conduct; codes of behavior	6
单词	dāncí	n.	vocabulary	6
单单	dāndān	adv.	only; solely	9
耽误	dānwu	v.	delay; make worse because of delay	8
胆小	dǎn xiǎo		timid	3
蛋糕	dàngāo	n.	cake	1
当初	dāngchū	t.	in the beginning; at first	10
当年	dāngnián	t.	that year (in the past)	5
导师	dǎoshī	n.	mentor; adviser	5
倒	dào	adv.	(indicating that sth. is not what one thinks)	2
倒是	dàoshì	adv.	but instead; used to express what is contrary to facts	10
道	dào	m.	(a measure word for lines, stripes, rainbows, etc.)	5
道理	dào·lǐ	n.	truth; reason	9
道歉	dào qiàn	vo.	apologize; make an apology	4
灯火	dēnghuǒ	n.	lights	5
登门	dēng mén	vo.	pay a visit to someone's house	3
地道	dìdao	adj.	genuine; authentic	1
地儿	dìr	n.	place (colloq.)	1
电汇	diànhuì	v.	transfer money telegraphically	9
调查	diàochá	v.	investigate	9
懂事	dǒng shì	vo.	be sensible; intelligent	10
动	dòng	v.	touch	10
兜	dōu	n.	pocket	2
兜（着）	dōu (zhe)	v.	(see note 11)	9
逗	dòu	adj./v.	amusing, funny; amuse	1
读研	dú yán	vo.	study as a graduate student	5
赌气	dǔ qì	vo.	feel wronged and act rashly	4
短信	duǎnxìn	n.	short message (on a cell phone)	7
段	duàn	m.	section; paragraph; passage	5
对口	duìkǒu	adj.	(see note 8)	7
对门	duìmén	n.	across the hallway; (of two apartments) facing each other	6
多事	duō shì	vo.	meddle	9

E

恶心	ěxin	adj. /v.	disgusting	10
饿	è	adj.	hungry	6
二十万	èrshí wàn	num.	two hundred thousand	9

F

发财	fā cái	vo.	get rich；make a fortune	7
发誓	fā shì	vo.	swear；vow	4
发现	fāxiàn	v.	find out	4
翻	fān	v.	turn over；turn up	4
反应过来	fǎnyìng guolai	vc.	realize	8
反正	fǎnzhèng	adv.	anyway；in any case	6
犯	fàn	v.	make (a mistake)；commit (a crime)	4
方式	fāngshì	n.	way；style	6
放心	fàng xīn	vo.	rest assured；not to worry	3
非要	fēi yào		must；be determined (to do something)	9
风土人情	fēng tǔ rén qíng		local costumes	6
夫人	fūren	n.	Mrs；wife	6
福尔摩斯	Fú'ěrmósī	n.	Sherlock Holmes (a detective in the works of the 19th-century English novelist Arthur Conan Doyle)	9
复试	fùshì	n.	re-exam；second-round exam	7
复制	fùzhì	v.	copy	5

G

该	gāi	adv.	ought to；should	4
改	gǎi	v.	change；correct	4
概念	gàiniàn	n.	concept	4
敢	gǎn	modal.	dare	3
感觉	gǎnjué	n.	feeling	5
赶紧	gǎnjǐn	adv.	hurry up	2
感谢	gǎnxiè	v.	thank for；be grateful for	7
干	gàn	v.	do；work	5
干吗	gànmá	pron.	for what；what to do (colloq.)	5
干吗	gànmá	pron.	why；what for	3
干什么	gàn shénme		why；what to do	3

刚好	gānghǎo	adj.	just right (as used in this story)	4
钢蹦儿	gāngbèngr	n.	coin (colloq.)	9
高声	gāo shēng		loud; loudly	7
高手	gāoshǒu	n.	master hand	5
高校	gāoxiào	n.	college; university	3
搞	gǎo	v.	make	3
搁	gē	v.	put; place	2
哥们儿	gēmenr	n.	buddy; pal (colloq.)	7
格调	gédiào	n.	style	9
根本	gēnběn	adv.	absolutely; fundamentally	9
公安局	gōng'ānjú	n.	police station; public security bureau	9
宫殿	gōngdiàn	n.	palace	1
工会	gōnghuì	n.	labor union; trade union	3
公交车	gōngjiāochē	n.	vehicle of public transportation	7
恭喜	gōngxǐ	v.	congratulate	7
共进晚餐	gòng jìn wǎncān		eat dinner together	6
共享	gòngxiǎng	v.	share; sharing	5
姑奶奶	gūnǎinai	n.	grandaunt	9
姑娘	gūniang	n.	girl; daughter	10
顾全大局	gùquán dàjú		(see note 9)	7
故宫	Gùgōng	N.	Imperial Palace	1
故事	gùshi	n.	story	1
故意	gùyì	adv.	intentionally; deliberately	8
挂	guà	v.	hang	5
挂炉	guàlú	n.	(a kind of stove for roasting duck)	1
乖	guāi	adj.	(of a child) obedient; well behaved; be good	4
怪	guài	adv.	very; quite	3
关系	guān·xì	n.	relation; relationship; relevance	7
管	guǎn	prep.	from (sb.)	2
光	guāng	adv.	only; merely	5
闺女	guīnü	n.	daughter	3
过不了	guò bu liǎo	vc.	unable to pass	3

H

咳	hāi	interj.	(an exclamation)	2
害	hài	v.	impair; cause trouble to	7

憨憨	Hānhān	N.	(name of a dog)	10
含蓄	hánxù	adj.	subtle; reserved	6
寒碜	hánchen	adj.	ugly	10
汉语	Hànyǔ	N.	Chinese language	1
好几天	hǎo jǐ tiān		quite a few days	2
好了	hǎo le		OK; that's enough	3
好日子	hǎo rìzi		auspicious date; happy occasion	3
好受	hǎoshòu	adj.	comfortable	5
好像	hǎoxiàng	v.	seem like	9
耗子	hàozi	n.	mouse; rat	7
荷兰	Hélán	N.	the Netherlands; Holland	7
河南	Hénán	N.	Henan (a province in China)	7
合同	hétong	n.	agreement; contract	9
嗨	hēi	interj.	(used to call attention) hey	8
嘿	hei	interj.	(used to call attention)	5
哼	hēng	interj.	Hmph	2
红烧	hóngshāo	v.	braise (meat)	2
后果	hòuguǒ	n.	consequence	9
后面	hòumian	n.	at the back; behind	2
壶	hú	n.	kettle; pot	2
花园	huāyuán	n.	garden	3
划拉	huála	v.	scribble	5
画外音	huà wài yīn	n.	off screen voice (in film or TV)	7
怀疑	huáiyí	v.	suspect; doubt	4
荒郊野外	huāngjiāo yěwài		wilderness	9
(上)回	(shàng) huí	m.	last time (same as 上次)	2
回首	huí shǒu	vo.	turn one's head; turn around (literary)	5
汇款	huìkuǎn	n./v.	remittance	9
汇票	huìpiào	n.	money order	9
混	hùn	v.	(see note 3)	7
活人	huórén	n.	living person	5

J

机会	jīhuì	n.	opportunity	7
记性	jìxing	n.	memory	4
计较	jìjiào	v.	discuss in minute detail; argue; dispute	8
既然	jìrán	conj.	since; now that	9

技术	jìshù	n.	technology; skill	7
寂寞	jìmò	adj.	lonely; lonesome	10
家	jiā	m.	(measure word for business establishments)	1
家常便饭	jiācháng biànfàn		homely food	6
家常菜	jiācháng cài	n.	homely dish	6
家具	jiājù	n.	furniture	9
家长	jiāzhǎng	n.	parent or guardian of a child	4
加起来	jiā qilai	vc.	total; add together	8
假	jiǎ	adj.	fake; false	8
假币	jiǎbì	n.	fake money; counterfeit	8
假不了	jiǎ bu liǎo	vc.	cannot be fake	8
假钱	jiǎ qián	n.	fake money	8
假装	jiǎzhuāng	v.	pretend	8
捡	jiǎn	v.	pick up	10
将	jiāng	prep.	(a more formal equivalent of the preposition 把)	9
讲	jiǎng	v.	pay attention to	2
讲究	jiǎngjiu	v. /n.	pay attention to; be particular about; be fussy about	1
交	jiāo	v.	hand in	5
叫法	jiàofǎ	n.	the way one addresses someone	10
教诲	jiàohuì	v.	teaching; instruction; advice	7
教师	jiàoshī	n.	teacher	1
教训	jiàoxun	v.	lesson	8
教育	jiàoyù	v.	teach; educate	4
街坊	jiēfang	n.	neighbor	10
接受	jiēshòu	v.	accept	6
结(了)婚	jié (le) hūn	vo.	get married	3
结了	jié le		(see note 11)	2
解馋	jiě chán	vo.	(see note 3)	2
斤	jīn	m.	of weight (equal to 1/2 kilogram)	8
今儿	jīnr	t.	today (colloq.)	1
进行	jìnxíng	v.	carry on; carry out; conduct	7
尽快	jǐnkuài	adv.	as quickly (soon) as possible	8
进入	jìnrù	v.	enter; get into	5
经常	jīngcháng	adv.	often; regularly	1

经理	jīnglǐ	n.	manager	7
精神	jīngshen	adj.	lively; vigorous	10
惊喜	jīngxǐ	n.	pleasant surprise	3
警察	jǐngchá	n.	police	9
净	jìng	adv.	purely; completely	3
竞争	jìngzhēng	v.	compete	7
句	jù	m.	(a measure word for speech)	6
距离	jùlí	n.	distance; disparity	7
据我所知	jù wǒ suǒ zhī		to my knowledge	5
句子	jùzl	n.	sentence	6
绝对	juéduì	adv.	Absolutely	4
绝了	jué le		beyond compare	5
觉着	juézhe	v.	feel	3

K

卡	kǎ	n.	card; credit card	9
开口	kāi kǒu	vo.	open one's mouth; start to talk	4
看法	kàn·fǎ	n.	opinion; point of view	5
看来	kàn lái		it appears; it seems	5
看重	kànzhòng	v.	value; think highly of	7
烤	kǎo	v.	bake; roast; toast; broil	1
考虑	kǎolǜ	v.	consider; think about	3
考验	kǎoyàn	v./n.	ordeal; test	7
烤鸭	kǎoyā	n.	roast duck	1
烤鸭店	kǎoyā diàn	n.	roast duck restaurant	1
肯定	kěndìng	adv.	certainly; definitely	2
吭	kēng	v.	utter a sound or a word	10
口味	kǒuwèi	n.	(of food) taste; flavor	1
夸张	kuāzhāng	adj.	exaggerated	10

L

拉	lā	v.	(of a driver) drive (somebody)	1
阑珊	lánshān	v.	waning; coming to an end (literary)	5
浪漫	làngmàn	adj.	romantic; unconventional	3
老板	lǎobǎn	n.	boss; manager; shopkeeper	8
老伴儿	lǎobànr	n.	husband or wife (of an old married couple)	2
老北京	lǎo běijīng		person who has lived in Beijing for a	1

long time and knows the city thoroughly

老公	lǎogōng	n.	husband (colloquial term)	10
老奶奶	lǎonǎinai	n.	grandmother; granny	10
老年	lǎonián	n.	(of a person) old; old age	7
老朋友	lǎo péngyou		old friend	1
老婆	lǎopó	n.	wife	6
老人家	lǎorénjiā	n.	(an respectful form of address for an old person)	3
老头子	lǎotóuzi	n.	old man, husband (wife's term of address for her old husband)	8
老兄	lǎoxiōng	n.	buddy; pal (colloq.)	7
老爷子	lǎoyézi	n.	old man; elderly person	8
老子	lǎozi	n.	father (colloquial expression)	4
姥姥	lǎolao	n.	(maternal) grandmother	4
了解	liǎojiě	v.	understand; know (sb) well	4
愣	lèng	adv.	insist on	9
厉害	lìhai	adj.	formidable; powerful	5
利用	lìyòng	v.	make use of; take advantage of	6
良师出高徒	liáng shī chū gāo tú		a great teachers produces brilliant students; the teacher of enlightenment brings up disciples of accomplishment	6
良心	liángxīn	n.	conscience	9
两口子	liǎngkǒuzi	n.	husband and wife; married couple	6
两下子	liǎng xiàzi		(see note 1)	9
邻居	línjū	n.	neighbor; people of the neighborhood	6
领(个)证	lǐng (ge) zhèng	vo.	apply the certificate; receive the certificate	3
令人失望	lìng rén shīwàng		disappointing	7
喽	lou	interj.	a sentence particle, same as 了 here	10
露两手	lòu liǎng shǒu		(see note 5)	6
炉火	lúhuǒ	n.	stove fire	1
录用	lùyòng	v.	employ; hire	7
乱	luàn	adj.	indiscriminately (as used in this context)	10
论文	lùnwén	n.	thesis; dissertation; paper	5
旅游	lǚyóu	v.	travel; tour	1

M

嘛	ma	part.	(used to emphasize the obvious)	2
麻利	máli	adj.	quick	3
满分	mǎn fēn		full score	5
慢用	màn yòng		eat casually; take your time	1
冒傻气	mào shǎqì	vo.	(see note 6)	2
没法	méi fǎ		unable	5
美食	měishí	n.	delicious food; delicacies	1
眛	mèi	v.	conceal	9
昧良心	mèi liángxīn	vo.	go against one's conscience	8
闷炉	mènlú	n.	(a kind of stove for roasting duck)	1
秘诀	mìjué	n.	secret of success; knack	5
秘书	mìshū	n.	secretary	7
面条儿	miàntiáor	n.	noodles	1
名吃	míngchī	n.	famous food	1
名片	míngpiàn	n.	business card	9
明白	míngbai	v./adj.	understand; come to see; clear	7
明明	míngmíng	adv.	obviously; simply	4
蓦然	mòrán	adv.	suddenly; abruptly	5
陌生	mòshēng	adj.	unknown; unfamiliar	7
陌生人	mòshēng rén	n.	stranger	3
某	mǒu	pron.	certain; indefinite (person or thing)	7
母亲	mǔqin	n.	mother	3
目击	mùjī	v.	witness	9

N

嗯	ǹ	interj.	(an exclamation)	3
拿走	ná zǒu	vc.	take away	9
哪儿有的事	nǎr yǒu de shì		that's nonsense	3
难道	nándào	adv.	Is it possible that...; Do you really mean to say that...	6
脑	nǎo	n.	brain; head	3
闹肚子	nào dùzi	vo.	have diarrhea	10
闹了半天	nào le bàn tiān		(see note 10)	10
能否	néng fǒu		possible or not; able or not; whether	7
能力	nénglì	n.	ability; talent	7

年纪轻	niánjì qīng		young	8
年轻	niánqīng	adj.	young	3
尿	niào	n.	urine	5
宁静	níngjìng	adj.	peaceful and tranquil	7
弄	nòng	v.	do; handle; deal with (colloq.)	5
弄丢	nòng diū	vc.	lose; mislay	5
女士	nǚshì	n.	lady; madam	6

O

| 噢 | ō | interj. | (suggesting surprised understanding) | 1 |
| 欧式 | ōushì | adj. | of European style | 9 |

P

排	pái	v.	rank	5
配	pèi	v.	match (color, style, etc.)	10
烹调	pēngtiáo	v.	cook	6
碰见	pèng jiàn	vc.	meet unexpectedly; run into	5
碰巧	pèngqiǎo	adj.	coincident	10
偏僻	piānpì	adj.	remote; out of the way	9
骗子	piànzi	n.	swindler; cheater	2
品位	pǐnwèi	n.	rank; grade; status	9
凭	píng	prep.	with (the authority or quality of)	7
平时	píngshí	t.	ordinarily; normally	10
评价	píngjià	v./n.	appraise, ssess; appraisal, assessment	5

Q

欺骗	qīpiàn	v.	cheat; deceive	5
妻子	qīzi	n.	wife	6
奇了怪了	qí le guài le		(see note 3)	6
其实	qíshí	adv.	as a matter of fact; actually	4
其中	qízhōng	n.	amid it; among them	5
起(什么)哄	qǐ (shénme) hòng	vo.	kick up a fuss; stir up a disturbance	7
岂有此理	qǐ yǒu cǐ lǐ		ridiculous; nonsense	10
钱	qián	n.	money	2
钱包	qiánbāo	n.	purse; wallet	2
抢	qiǎng	v.	fight (with someone over something, as used in this story)	10

瞧	qiáo		look	2
瞧好儿吧	qiáo hǎor bā		(see note 2)	8
憔悴	qiáocuì	adj.	haggard，sallow；pined away	5
青年	qīngnián	n.	youth；young person	9
轻巧	qīng•qiǎo	adj.	simple；easy	2
青青	Qīngqīng	N.	(a nickname for Lü Qing)	9
轻易	qīngyì	adv.	easily；lightly	5
清香	qīngxiāng	adj.	delicately fragrant	1
情书	qíngshū	n.	love letter	5
情调	qíngdiào	n.	sentiment；taste	3
请勿	qǐng wù		please do not (literary)	7
求	qiú	v.	beg	10
取证	qǔ zhèng	vo.	collect evidence	9
全	quán	adv.	completely；entirely	7
全部	quánbù		totality；entirety	3
全聚德	Quánjùdé	N.	(name of a restaurant)	1
全选	quán xuǎn		select all	5
缺	quē	v.	be short of；lack	4

R

确实	quèshí	adv.	indeed；truly	9
热情	rèqíng	adj.	passionate；warm-hearted	1
人才	réncái	n.	person of ability and talent	7
人家	rénjia	pron.	sb. else；other people	2
人品	rénpǐn	n.	moral character	7
认错	rèn cuò	vo.	admit a mistake；apologize	4
认真	rènzhēn	adj.	serious	2
任何	rènhé	pron.	any	7
扔	rēng	v.	throw；throw away	9
日子	rìzi	n.	day；days	2
肉铺	ròupù	n.	meat shop	8
如此	rúcǐ	pron.	such；this kind of	5

S

嗓门儿	sǎngménr	n.	voice	7
啥	shá	pron.	what；whatever	7
商量	shāngliang	v.	discuss；talk over with sb.	2

上车	shàng chē	vo.	get in the car (or on the bus or train)	1
上当	shàng dàng	vo.	be fooled	8
上缴	shàngjiǎo	v.	turn over (to a higher authority)	8
捎	shāo	v.	send (a message)	3
舍友	shèyǒu	n.	dormmate; roommate	5
什么的	shénme de...		etC.	10
生气	shēng qì	vo.	angry; get angry	5
声音	shēngyīn	n.	voice; sound	7
盛	chéng	v.	fill	2
失去	shīqù	v.	lose; miss	7
失主	shīzhǔ	n.	owner (of the lost item)	9
时代	shídài	n.	age; era; epoch	5
实话跟您说	shíhuà gēn nín shuō		tell you the truth	1
实在	shízài	adj./adv.	true; honest	6
食品	shípǐn	n.	food	1
时尚	shíshàng	n.	fashion; vogue	9
使	shǐ	v.	use; employ	2
市场	shìchǎng	n.	market; marketplace	8
市场管理处	shìchǎng guǎnlǐchù		Market Management Department	8
事先	shìxiān	t.	in advance; beforehand	3
收据	shōujù	n.	receipt	9
首	shǒu	n.	head; first place	5
手包	shǒubāo	n.	handbag; purse	9
守寡	shǒu guǎ	vo.	live in widowhood	3
手机	shǒujī	n.	cell phone	7
手艺	shǒuyì	n.	skill; craftsmanship	6
守着	shǒu zhe		(see note 6)	6
寿星老儿	shòuxīnglǎor	n.	person whose birthday is being celebrated	1
叔叔	shūshu	n.	(child's form of address for any young man of one generation its senior) uncle; father's younger brother	10
舒心	shūxīn	adj.	pleasant	7
属于	shǔyú	v.	belong to	3
涮羊肉	shuàn yángròu		instant boiled mutton	1
水平	shuǐpíng	n.	level; proficiency; sophistication	5
说不过	shuō bu guò	vc.	not as eloquent as...	10
说道	shuōdao	v.	discuss	8

说理	shuō lǐ	vo.	argue；dispute	8
说明	shuōmíng	v.	denote；demonstrate	9
说清楚	shuō qīngchu	vc.	make clear；state clearly	8
司机	sījī	n.	driver；chauffeur	1
死活	sǐhuó	adv.	anyway；no matter what	4
送过去	sòng guoqu	vc.	deliver/carry (something over)	4
素质	sùzhì	n.	quality；character	7
算错账	suàn cuò zhàng		add the sum wrong	8
随便	suíbiàn	adv.	random，casual；randomly，casually	5
随地大小便	suídì dàxiǎobiàn		relieve (oneself) anywhere	10
岁数	suìshu	n.	age	8
锁	suǒ	v./n.	lock	2

T

踏实	tāshi	adj.	feel at ease；steadfast	2
摊儿	tānr	n.	stall；vendor's stand by a road or on a square	2
趟	tàng	m.	(measure word for a trip)	8
淘汰	táotài	v.	eliminate through selection；discard	9
提	tí	v.	mention about	2
题目	tímù	n.	topic	5
体现	tǐxiàn	v.	embody；reflect	9
替	tì	prep.	take the place of；substitue for	1
天空	tiānkōng	n.	sky	5
天真	tiānzhēn	adj.	naïve	9
条件	tiáojiàn	n.	situation；environment	6
挑战	tiǎozhàn	v./n.	challenge	7
听不见	tīng bu jiàn	vc.	unable to hear；inaudible	7
听懂	tīng dǒng	vc.	understand	6
听见	tīng jiàn	vc.	hear	7
挺	tǐng	adv.	very；rather	2
通过	tōngguò	v.	pass；succeed in (an exam；etc.)	7
同事	tóngshì	n.	colleague；co-worker；workmate	3
偷	tōu	v.	steal	4
透气	tòu qì	vo.	get fresh air	10
退一步说	tuì yí bù shuō		(see note 6)	9
托	tuō	v.	entrust (somebody to do something)	5

妥协	tuǒxié	v.	compromise	10

W

哇啦哇啦	wāla wāla		(an onomatopoeia for loud voice)	7
外焦里嫩	wài jiāo lǐ nèn		burnt outside but tender inside	1
外教	wàijiào	n.	foreign teacher	6
外面	wài · miàn	n.	outside	2
外语	wàiyǔ	n.	foreign language	6
完全	wánquán	adv.	complete，whole；completely，wholly	5
万一	wànyī	adv.	in case	3
汪	wāng	ono.	(onomatopoeia；sound that dogs make)	4
网络	wǎngluò	n.	internet；network	5
胃口	wèikǒu	n.	appetite	1
未来	wèilái	n.	future	7
文章	wénzhāng	n.	writing	5
文字	wénzì	n.	written words；writing	5
吻合	wěnhé	adj.	consistent with	7
无论	wúlùn	conj.	whether... or...	5

X

西瓜	xīguā	n.	watermelon	3
喜新厌旧	xǐ xīn yàn jiù		(see note 2)	10
细	xì	adj.	fine；thin	1
细说	xì shuō		say in detail	5
瞎	xiā	adv.	groundlessly；foolishly	2
下班	xià bān	vo.	get off work	2
下文	xiàwén	n.	(see note 8)	2
下载	xiàzài	v.	download	5
吓唬	xiàhu	v.	frighten；scare	3
夏令营	xiàlìngyíng	n.	summer camp	4
吓着	xià zhao	vc.	frighten	10
先斩后奏	xiān zhǎn hòu zòu		(see note 7)	3
嫌弃	xiánqì	v.	dislike and avoid；disfavor	10
闲事	xiánshì	n.	other people's business	7
现场	xiànchǎng	n.	scene (of event or incident)；site；spot	9
现成	xiànchéng	adj.	readily available	6
香	xiāng	adj.	delicious	6

相信	xiāngxìn	v.	believe	9
想起	xiǎng qǐ	vc.	think of; recall	5
想起来	xiǎng qilai	vc.	recall; remember	2
像…似的	xiàng…shìde		be like...	3
象征	xiàngzhēng	v.	symbolize; signify	1
消	xiāo	v.	become thinner (literary)	5
消停	xiāoting	adj.	calm; uneventful	9
小狗	xiǎogǒu	n.	little dog	4
小伙子	xiǎohuǒzi	n.	lad; young fellow	2
小气鬼	xiǎoqìguǐ	n.	mean person (as used in this story); miser	10
小气劲儿	xiǎoqi jìnr		stingy; miserly	4
小声	xiǎoshēng	adv.	(speak) softly; whisper	7
小偷儿	xiǎotōur	n.	petty thief	9
小心	xiǎoxīn	v./adj.	be careful; be cautious	10
小夜曲	xiǎoyèqǔ	n.	serenade	9
笑话	xiàohua	v./n.	laugh at;joke	4
心里	xīnli		in the heart; in the mind	2
心疼	xīnténg	v.	love dearly; feel sorry	2
心眼儿	xīnyǎnr	n.	intelligence; cleverness	2
信儿	xìnr	n.	message	3
信誉	xìnyù	n.	reputation	2
兴	xīng	v.	have (something) in vogue	1
行了	xíng le		enough of it; stop it	5
刑事	xíngshì	adj.	criminal	9
形象	xíngxiàng	n.	image	7
幸福	xìngfú	adj./n.	happy; happiness	3
凶	xiōng	adj.	vicious; fierce; mean	10
兄弟	xiōngdi	n.	(see note 12)	7
修车	xiū chē	vo.	repair bike; fix bike	2
修养	xiūyǎng	n.	cultivation	7
许多	xǔduō	num.	many; much; a lot of	7
喧哗	xuānhuá	v.	make hubbub; make uproar	7
学会	xué huì	vc.	learn; master	6
学问	xuéwen	n.	learning; knowledge; scholarship	5

Y

鸭子	yāzi	n.	duck; duckling	1
邀请	yāoqǐng	v.	invite	6
摇上	yáo shàng	vc.	roll (a window) up (to close the window of a car)	10
要	yào	modal.	must	5
要不	yàobù	conj.	otherwise; or else	6
要面子	yào miànzi	vo.	be concerned about face saving; be sensitive about one's reputation	4
要求	yāoqiú	v.	requirement	7
钥匙	yàoshi	n.	key	2
爷爷	yéye	n.	(paternal) grandfather; grandpa	10
也许	yěxǔ	adv.	perhaps; probably; maybe	9
业务	yèwù	n.	vocational work; professional work	7
伊	yī	pron.	she; her (archaic)	5
一百万	yìbǎiwàn	num.	a million	9
一气	yí qì		(see note 13)	10
一切	yíqiè	pron.	all; everything	7
一万	yíwàn	num.	ten thousand	9
一直	yìzhí	adv.	always; all along	3
遗憾	yíhàn	adj.	regret; regrettable	5
以后	yǐhòu	t.	from now on; later on	6
意见	yì·jiàn	n.	view; opinion	3
意犹未尽	yì yóu wèi jìn		not having one's meaning/emotion fully expressed	5
因小失大	yīn xiǎo shī dà		(see note 11)	7
影响	yǐngxiǎng		impair; interfere with; affect	7
应聘	yìngpìn	v.	apply (for a job)	7
哟	yō	interj.	(expressing slight surprise)	1
由	yóu	prep.	up to (somebody to do something)	7
游	yóu	v.	tour; sightsee	1
游客	yóukè	n.	traveller; tourist; sightseer	1
油亮	yóuliàng	adj.	shiny; glossy	1
犹犹豫豫	yóu yóu yù yù	adj.	hesitant	3
有必要	yǒu bìyào	vo.	necessary	4
有点儿	yǒudiǎnr	adv.	a little bit; somewhat	1

有损	yǒusǔn	v.	harm; damage	7
有学问	yǒu xuéwen		knowledgeable	1
友好	yǒuhǎo	adj.	friendly	6
与	yǔ	conj.	and (literary)	7
遇到	yù dào	vc.	encounter; meet	9
郁闷	yùmèn	adj.	gloomy, depressed; be gloomy, be depressed	5
育新小区	Yùxīn Xiǎoqū	n.	Yuxin Subdivision	10
冤枉	yuānwang	v.	accuse (sb) wrongly	2
圆	yuán	adj.	round	1
员工	yuángōng	n.	employee; staff member	7
原来	yuánlái	adv./adj.	(it) turns out	10
原谅	yuánliàng	v.	forgive; pardon	4
月饼	yuèbing	n.	moon cake	1
月亮	yuèliang	n.	the moon	1
月票	yuèpiào	n.	monthly pass (for public transportation)	7
晕车	yùn chē	vo.	carsick	10

Z

咱	zán	pron.	we, us; I, me	1
咱家	zán jiā		my (as used in this story)	10
咱俩	zán liǎ		two of us	3
咱们	zánmen	pron.	we; us (including the listener)	1
早晨	zǎochén	t.	morning	2
责任	zérèn	n.	responsibility	9
怎么了	zěnme le		What happened? What's the matter?	2
怎么卖	zěnme mài		How much?	8
怎么着	zěnmezhe	pron.	what happened?	5
炸酱面	zhájiàngmiàn	n.	noodles in fried bean sauce	1
粘贴	zhāntiē	v.	paste	5
站名	zhànmíng	n.	name of the bus stop or railroad station	7
掌握	zhǎngwò	v.	grasp; master	6
招呼	zhāohu	v./n.	greet; greeting	6
找错	zhǎo cuò	vc.	look for (somebody or something) at a wrong place; arrive at a wrong place	3
找错门	zhǎo cuò mén		come to a wrong door	3

赵叔/	Zhào shū/	N.	Uncle Zhao	3
赵叔叔	Zhào shūshū			
这会儿	zhè huìr		now; at the moment	8
这么着	zhèmezhe	pron.	in that case	1
这哪儿跟哪儿	zhè nǎr gēn nǎr		(see note 10)	9
着急	zháojí	adj.	worried; anxious	2
着呢	zhene	part.	(following an adjective to indicate degree) very; quite; greatly	1
真诚	zhēnchéng	adj.	sincere; earnest	5
正	zhèng	adv.	right in the middle of (an action or a state)	5
正好	zhènghǎo	adv.	coindentally	8
证据	zhèngjù	n.	evidence; proof	8
证人	zhèng·rén	n.	witness	9
挣	zhèng	v.	earn	2
之	zhī	part.	(archaic and literary form for 的 indicating a possessive relationship)	5
知错就改	zhī cuò jiù gǎi		correct a mistake as soon as one realizes it	4
直接	zhíjiē	adj.	direct	6
值钱	zhíqián	adj.	valuable	9
纸	zhǐ	n.	paper	9
指不定	zhǐbudìng	adv.	perhaps; maybe	4
至于	zhìyú	v.	there is no need; not necessary	2
中国通	Zhōngguó tōng	n.	old China hand	1
猪肉	zhūròu	n.	pork	8
追不上	zhuī bu shàng	vc.	cannot catch up (with someone)	10
仔细	zǐxì	adj.	careful; cautious	8
资料	zīliào	n.	data; information	7
自然	zìrán	adv./adj.	normally; certainly	10
自私	zìsī	adj.	selfish; self-centered	3
综合	zōnghé	v.	comprehensive	7
总	zǒng	adv.	always	4
走人	zǒu rén	vo.	leave	8
琢磨	zuómo	v.	ponder; think over	2
做法	zuò·fǎ	n.	way of doing or making something	1
坐过了站	zuò guò le zhàn		(of a bus rider) miss the stop	7
坐好	zuò hǎo	vc.	get seated properly	1
做回主	zuò huí zhǔ	vo.	make the decision for (somebody)	1

做人	zuò rén	vo.	conduct oneself	2
做生意	zuò shēngyi	vo.	do business	8
做小买卖	zuò xiǎo mǎimai	vo.	do small business；do little trading	8
作者	zuòzhě	n.	writer；author	5
作证	zuò zhèng	vo.	testify；serve as witness	9

附录二：注释索引 Notes Index